MW00780909

Who Runs?

To explain women's underrepresentation in American politics, researchers have directed their attention to differences between men and women, especially during the candidate emergence process, which includes recruitment, perception of qualifications, and political ambition. Although these previous analyses have shown that consistent dissimilarities likely explain why men outnumber women in government, they have overlooked a more explicit role for gender (masculinity and femininity) in explanations of candidate emergence variation.

Sarah Oliver and Meredith Conroy focus on the candidate emergence process and investigate the effects of individuals' gender personality on these variables to improve theories of women's underrepresentation in government. They argue that because politics and masculinity are congruent, we should observe more precise variation in the candidate emergence process along gender differences, rather than along sex differences in isolation. Individuals who are more masculine will be more likely to be recruited, perceive of themselves as qualified, and express political ambition than will less masculine individuals. This differs from studies that look at sex differences, because it accepts that some women defy gender norms and break into politics. By including a measure of gender personality we can more fully grapple with women's progress in American politics, and consider whether this progress rests on masculine behaviors and attributes. *Who Runs? The Masculine Advantage in Candidate Emergence* explores this possibility and the potential ramifications.

Sarah Oliver is Assistant Professor of Political Science at Towson University.

Meredith Conroy is Associate Professor of Political Science at California State University, San Bernardino.

CAWP Series in Gender and American Politics

SERIES EDITORS:
Susan J. Carroll, Rutgers University
Kira Sanbonmatsu, Rutgers University

Center for American Women and Politics
Eagleton Institute of Politics   Rutgers University
www.cawp.rutgers.edu

WHO RUNS?

*The Masculine Advantage
in Candidate Emergence*

Sarah Oliver and Meredith Conroy

University of Michigan Press
Ann Arbor

Copyright © 2020 by Sarah Oliver and Meredith Conroy
All rights reserved

For questions or permissions, please contact um.press.perms@umich.edu

Published in the United States of America by the
University of Michigan Press
Manufactured in the United States of America
Printed on acid-free paper
First published July 2020

A CIP catalog record for this book is available from the British Library.

Library of Congress Cataloging-in-Publication Data

Names: Oliver, Sarah (Political scientist), author. | Conroy, Meredith, author.
Title: Who runs? : the masculine advantage in candidate emergence / Sarah Oliver and
    Meredith Conroy.
Description: Ann Arbor : University of Michigan Press, 2020. | Series: The CAWP series
    in gender and American politics | Includes bibliographical references and index. |
Identifiers: LCCN 2020016819 (print) | LCCN 2020016820 (ebook) |
    ISBN 9780472132102 (hardcover) | ISBN 9780472127092 (ebook)
Subjects: LCSH: Women political candidates. | Women—Political activity. | Sexism in
    political culture.
Classification: LCC HQ1236 .O45   2020 (print) | LCC HQ1236 (ebook) |
    DDC 320.082—dc23
LC record available at https://lccn.loc.gov/2020016819
LC ebook record available at https://lccn.loc.gov/2020016820

Cover image: Shutterstock.com / Patcharanan

Contents

Digital materials related to this title can be found on
the Fulcrum platform via the following citable URL:
https://doi.org/10.3998/mpub.10170475

Acknowledgments

This book wouldn't be possible without several people whom we would like to thank. We thank Caroline Heldman for shaping the way we think about gender and politics. As undergraduates, we both took courses from Caroline and worked as her research assistants on related projects. To say Caroline planted the seed for this, and our other, work would be an understatement.

We also thank Kira Sanbonmatsu for her guidance and mentorship with this project. Kira provided comments on various chapters of this book at various stages of the process that greatly improved our manuscript. Sue Carroll gave us encouraging feedback on our book proposal, and we thank her for taking the time to engage with our work. Thank you to the "Resisting Women's Political Leadership: Theories, Data, Solutions" Conference at Rutgers University in 2017, where the motivation to write this book took hold. Special thanks to conference participants Mona Lena Krook, Alice Eagly, and Kelly Dittmar. Thank you also to John McTague for reading chapters and providing feedback.

We appreciate Elizabeth Demers, with University of Michigan Press, who shepherded this manuscript from proposal status to the final product. We also appreciate the anonymous reviewers who provided thorough, constructive comments, alongside enthusiasm for this book. Danielle Coty and Haley Winkle with University of Michigan Press provided excellent assistance through the publishing process.

Thank you to the University of California, Santa Barbara, Social Science Survey Center, and especially Paolo Gardinali, for fielding our survey. Funding for the survey and preliminary research was provided by the Brython Davis Fellowship and the Political Science Department at the University of California, Santa Barbara. A special thanks to Eric R. A. N. Smith and M. Kent Jennings for help revising the survey and for many methodology discussions.

In addition, Sarah would like to thank Eric R. A. N. Smith and M. Kent Jennings for mentorship and encouragement. This book project started as a dissertation and would not have gotten to this point without both of you. Thank you for all the times you said "save it for the book." Well, here it is. Thank you also to Garrett Glasgow and Lorelei Moosbrugger for feedback and comments on early stages of the project. Sarah also appreciates the support from St. Lawrence University and Towson University, especially Grace Huang, Patty Ashlaw, Cindy Cates, and Mike Korzi. Additional thanks to Michael Zhang, Mario Serrano, Cameron Schunk, and Joanna Morganelli, who each worked as research assistants on this project. Thank you to Meredith. This book would not have been possible without your brilliant ideas and hard work. On a personal note, Sarah would like to thank her family and friends, especially Kelly Marine, Jeanne Oliver, and Patricia Kenitz. Also, to her cats, Eclipse and Heidi.

In addition to those already named, Meredith would like to thank Rosalee Clawson, M. Kent Jennings, Bruce Bimber, Lori Cox Han, and Justin Vaughn for years of encouragement and mentorship. She also thanks her supportive colleagues at California State University, San Bernardino. In particular, the department chair, Brian Janiskee, who helped Meredith balance teaching and research obligations while working on this book. Meredith would also like to thank her coauthor, Sarah Oliver, whose insights, creativity, and flexibility made writing this book a smooth and enjoyable process. Last, Meredith is indebted to her friends and family for their support.

Figures

Tables

ONE

Gender, Power, and Political Ambition

Since President Donald Trump's inauguration in January 2017, tens of thousands of women have expressed their interest in running for political office at all levels of government. According to Emily's List, one of the country's leading interest groups directed at recruiting and encouraging women to run for office, around 26,000 women expressed interest in running between 2017 and 2018 (Alter 2018). This interest among women translated into a surge in women-led candidacies, especially among Democrats (Conroy 2018a). In 2018, there was an 88 percent increase in women running for Congress from the previous midterm year (fig. 1.1). Media reports dubbed the phenomenon the "Pink Wave" (e.g., Haslett 2018; Goodkind 2018), and there was no shortage of articles declaring 2018 "The New 'Year of the Woman.'"

Of those women running in 2018, many of the more publicized were elevated by their political advertisements wherein they reenacted how they had overcome obstacles in traditionally male fields to find success in arenas where women have been historically left out, like the military. In these cases, the candidates rely on their military credentials to emphasize their association with masculine skills and traits in their advertising. Their ads are useful for understanding how sex and gender intersect, in an observable way, to convey candidate experience and qualification.

Take, for instance, U.S. Marine Corps veteran Amy McGrath, who ran for a congressional seat in Kentucky in 2018. In one of her ads, "Told Me," McGrath walks in front of a fighter jet on a landing strip in a bomber jacket, while describing her childhood goal to fly fighter jets, "the toughest

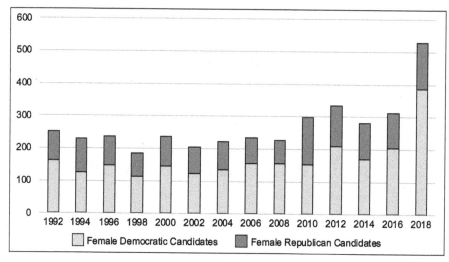

Fig. 1.1. Women Candidates in Republican and Democratic Congressional Primary Races, 1992–2018

(Data is from the Center for American Women in Politics at Rutgers University, "2018 Summary of Women Candidates" and "Women Candidates in 1992–2016: A Summary of Major Party Primary Candidates for U.S. Senate, U.S. House.")

flying you can do," and that her senator, Mitch McConnell, told her she couldn't do it. In the ad, McGrath explains she went on to fly in combat missions, and was the first woman to fly an F-18. As a Marine, McGrath flew 89 combat missions; in subsequent ads, she describes running for Congress as her 90th.

In Texas, Iraq war veteran MJ Hegar produced her ad, "Doors." The most prominent door in the ad is from Hegar's helicopter, which crash landed when she was a combat search and rescue pilot in Afghanistan; it was in that helicopter that Hagar was shot, but continued with the mission to get the injured soldiers to safety. In the ad, other doors feature prominently, and in most cases are shut in Hegar's face. Despite doors closing on Hegar, she found a way to overcome, by "opening, pushing, and sometimes kicking through every door that was in [her] way." For example, as she explains in the ad, after Hegar was discharged she filed a lawsuit against the Pentagon for their ban on women serving in ground combat jobs; she won her lawsuit, which opened the door for women after her to serve their country. Unsurprisingly, both of these ads went viral (Kruse 2018), boasting views in the millions, and contributing handsomely to the candidates' campaign coffers (e.g., Ratcliffe 2018).

Ads like these draw attention and praise for a couple of reasons. First, they champion an underdog who overcame obstacles and barriers to reach her goals. Second, they showcase a woman willing to break free from stereotypes about women as soft-spoken caretakers, and display qualities, characteristics, and experiences that are masculine and not traditionally feminine. In this manner, candidates like McGrath and Hegar remind us that women are multifaceted and that women cannot be shoehorned into conventional notions of womanhood.

However, a more pessimistic view of ads like these is that less masculine women view the political landscape as one that is unfriendly to their strengths and are less likely to jump in the fray, especially at higher levels. Certainly, women campaign by emphasizing a variety of experiences and skills (e.g., Carpinella and Bauer 2019). For instance, in her primary race for governor in Wisconsin, Democratic candidate Kelda Helen Roys breastfed her new baby in her ad while discussing her plan to protect children from toxic chemicals. Another example from 2018 is Lauren Underwood who ran for Congress in Illinois by emphasizing her experiences as a nurse and caring for other people, in a compassion-centered campaign. Indeed, campaigns make the decision to invoke masculine or feminine traits and issues, or both, using visual and rhetorical cues (e.g., Dittmar 2015b; Carpinella and Bauer 2019), to varying success (e.g. Bauer 2017, 2018a, 2018b, 2019; Schneider 2014). But beneath the choice to invoke gender cues in advertising and campaigning is an individuals' extant possession of gender personality traits. Does gender personality help explain whether an individual is willing and wanting to run for higher office? Our answer, briefly, is yes, individuals who possess more masculine personalities are at an advantage.

Running for office is one of the costliest forms of political participation individuals can engage in, and the decision to run for office is complex and complicated. Political science scholarship on this topic is broad and deep. In terms of breadth, studies span from interviews with elected officials about whether they will run for higher office, a concept referred to as *progressive ambition* (e.g., Carroll 1985; Carroll and Sanbonmatsu 2013; Sweet-Cushman 2018), to surveys of the mass public that ask whether individuals have ever considered running, a concept referred to as *nascent ambition* (e.g., Crowder-Meyer 2018; Lawless and Fox 2010; Holman and Schneider 2018). In terms of depth, these studies consider structural, situational, and psychological factors that mediate and moderate the decision to run for office. Most of this scholarship finds men's and women's orientation to, and perception of, politics varies in ways that helps explain why women are less likely than men to express both nascent and progressive ambition.

Implicit in much of the previous scholarship is evidence of a more explicit role for gender personality (masculinity and femininity) to explain candidate emergence and political ambition variation. It is these implicit mechanisms that we intend to draw out in this book, as we bridge the gap between (a) studies that focus on differences between men and women and (b) theories about the role of gender—masculinity and femininity—to more fully appreciate the intersection of gender and sex; together, gender and sex can help explain political behavior, like running for political office.

Our argument is that variation in successfully navigating the candidate emergence process is tied closely to gender, and that individuals with more masculine personalities, irrespective of their sex, are more likely to perceive of themselves as qualified, be recruited, and therefore express interest in running for higher political office. This is because the process of candidate emergence itself is gendered. Recruitment channels are masculine—recruiters still largely draw from masculine fields like business and legal professions (e.g., Crowder-Meyer and Lauderdale 2014); notions of what it means to be qualified are masculine—leadership is still widely perceived to necessitate masculine qualities (e.g., Koenig et al. 2011; Lawless 2004; Sanbonmatsu and Dolan 2009; Huddy and Terkildsen 1993; Godbole, Malvar, and Valian 2019); and aspirations that a political career satisfies, like status and power, are more masculine goals (e.g., Schneider et al. 2016). While these conditions typically benefit men, women can, and do, successfully run for political office, despite what we argue is an uneven, gendered playing field. Indeed, by and large, masculinity is more congruent with American politics than femininity, which contributes to the belief—externalized and internalized—that women are less compatible with positions of political power and influence than men. This raises an interesting question: Should we expect women who identify with personality traits that break from gender stereotypes to also break into politics more easily? We suggest that this is likely to bear out.

A Theory of Gender Personality and Progressive Political Ambition

In this book, we build on past scholarship interested in the incompatibility between women and politics by drawing more attention to how the incompatibility is based in notions of gender personality—masculinity and femininity. While recent scholarship has grappled with gender in theory and empirically, we extend this work to identify how gender is manifested psychologically to influence the road to candidate emergence and progres-

women are making by breaking into political institutions—which should certainly be celebrated—women's success in electoral politics still largely demands that they be compatible with the preconceived ideas about leadership as masculine, and assume the preworn paths to political leadership that prefer masculinity. Therefore, we anticipate that those who do not identify with primarily masculine personality traits will be less likely to emerge as candidates for higher political office.

Studying Gender Differences versus Studying Sex Differences

We define sex and gender as analytically distinct measures of different phenomena. Georgia Duerst-Lahti and Rita Mae Kelly (1995, 15) argued that "to assume equality between men and women by making them equal categories is to predetermine the outcome of analysis" and that looking at sex as an analytical category "does not facilitate analyzing the way gender is entangled with social resources—such as control of major institutions, wealth, and knowledge and the way they have been maldistributed between the sexes." Their primary claim is that to understand this maldistribution of resources, and the power imbalance that arises, more attention needs to be paid to gender. While studying differences between men and women is important to understanding the political landscape, especially since numerous gaps in political phenomena exist between men and women, to explain political phenomena social scientists should also attempt to parse the ways that gender intersects with sex (e.g., McDermott 2016). "Gender" is available to people of any sex; however, societal expectations exist about when particular gender behaviors are appropriate, and for whom.

Indeed, decades of scholarship in political science have made the distinction between sex and gender, and more recent studies have worked to empirically measure them as unique. For example, studies on gender stereotypes incorporate masculinity and femininity into studies of perceptions of men and women. Studies look at whether individuals perceive male and female candidates uniquely in possession of masculine and feminine traits, and masculine and feminine issue expertise, respectively (e.g., Dolan 2014; Dolan and Lynch 2014). Building on this, experimental designs assess whether associations with feminine and masculine traits and issues affect perceptions of male and female candidates, a concept referred to as "gender bending" (Schneider 2014; Bauer 2018a, 2018b; Bauer and Carpinella 2018). From this body of work, which we review more fully in chapter 2, we have come to better understand how gender stereotypes manifest in evaluations of political candidates, and whether individuals are more or less biased against female candidates in the abstract, and women in certain contexts, due to these associations.

But gender stereotypes are also internalized. Through the framework of social role theory, segregated social roles of women and men lead to gender stereotypic behavior and attitudes by women and men (Diekman and Eagly 2000; Wood and Eagly 2002; see Schneider and Bos 2019 for review). According to social role theory, segregation of men and women into different occupational roles in society has led men and women to observe and adopt particular traits and personalities; men tend to adopt more agentic traits (masculine) and women tend to adopt more communal traits (feminine) (Diekman and Eagly 2000; Wood and Eagly 2002). As Schneider and Bos (2019, 177) summarize,

> In short, being assigned male at birth results in the adoption of agentic traits and roles because boys observe men doing so, they are rewarded for such decisions, and they are likely to develop an identity associated with agency (e.g., Wood and Eagly 2012). The same process occurs for girls and women with regard to communal traits and roles.

Although women tend to identify with more feminine traits and men with more masculine traits, variation in personality adoption and expression occur *among* women and men. Shifting social norms and individual-level experiences will lead to variation in the degree to which social roles are seen as male- or female-typical. Thus, although women are more likely to identify with communal traits and possess communal goals, and men are more likely to identify with agentic traits and possess agentic goals, men and women can and do vary in their possession of both (Twenge 1997, 2001; Spence and Buckner 2000). As such, variation in political behaviors may correspond with agentic and communal traits and goals among men and women (e.g., McDermott 2016; Schneider et al. 2016).

For instance, McDermott (2016) assessed the impact of gender personality on mass political behavior and party identification. In looking at individual-level differences in political behavior, McDermott (2016) challenges the long-standing "gender gaps" that are attributed to differences between men and women by assessing the role of gender personality. McDermott measures individuals' identification with masculinity and femininity using personality tests, and finds that feminine and masculine personality dimensions strongly influence partisan identification, vote choice, and ideology. She concludes that masculinity's effect on political behaviors is stronger than individuals' sex. In this book, we extend gender personality to an additional political behavior—the decision to run for higher office.

Gender and Power

We present our argument through the lens of gendered power, where masculinity provides privileges in American politics, and these privileges are better afforded to any potential candidate who possesses a masculine personality, regardless of sex. So long as the process of candidate emergence is masculine, masculine individuals will be more successful at navigating this process. This maintenance of masculinized politics, despite women's progress in terms of descriptive representation, suggests that electing more women to office may not be enough to overturn the centuries-long bias toward masculinized norms, standards, and knowledge, biases that largely benefit men.

A gender hierarchy exists in American politics. It is manifest in the institutionalization of norms, codes, legitimacy, and knowledge that largely benefit men (King 1995; Anderson and Sheeler 2005). A gender hierarchy is a system that values characteristics of a particular gender more than another gender, and rewards behaviors and attributes associated with that gender such that it is prioritized, and elevated, maintaining a status differentiation. Studies on leadership find ample evidence of a gender hierarchy where masculinity is more valued. According to a meta-analysis of three psychological research paradigms interested in leadership and stereotypes of men and women, descriptions of leaders, professionals, and managers reflect masculine characteristics, qualities, and behaviors (Koenig et al. 2011). The same is true for political leadership, especially the presidency (Godbole, Malvar, and Valian 2019; Beail, Goren, and McHugh 2019).

In elections, candidates of any sex derive power by upholding norms of masculinity, reinforcing the gender hierarchy in American politics. This phenomenon was on display during the 2016 Republican primary, when the mostly male candidates openly targeted their opponents by casting them as not manly enough. For instance, former Texas governor Rick Perry challenged Donald Trump to a pull-up contest, which is essentially a contest about manhood (Schleifer 2015); Trump repeated an audience member's comment that Senator Ted Cruz was a "pussy" (Johnson 2016); Trump called Senator Marco Rubio "Little Marco" (Dicker 2016); Rubio suggested that Trump had a small penis when he said "you know what they say about guys with small hands" (Jaffe 2016); and an art collective, Indecline, installed a series of statues featuring a naked Donald Trump with a micropenis and no

balls in large cities around the United States. Indecline entitled the installation *The Emperor Has No Balls* (Garber-Paul 2016). The problem with this
seemingly radical installation is the underlying theme that feminized men
are less fit to lead. That Trump is without his balls unwittingly elevates masculinity in the presidential contest at the expense of femininity.

Operating within the framework that masculinity is a virtue and femininity is a vice, men running for president have long been feminized by
their opponents to exploit the unconscious incongruence between femininity and presidential leadership. For example, in 1988, Michael Dukakis's
tank ride feminized him in a way that made him appear unfit for the presidency in the eyes of many. Once a video surfaced of the Democratic nominee looking diminutive in an enormous tank, wearing an oversized helmet
with his name stenciled across the front, the Bush campaign worked tire-
lessly to keep the image in the press. In one ad, the Bush campaign went
after Dukakis's military and national security positions and looped footage
of the tank ride with the message, "Now he wants to be our commander in
chief? America can't afford that risk" (King 2013).

George H. W. Bush was also feminized during the 1988 campaign.
Before he formally announced he was running for president, *Newsweek*
magazine ran a cover story entitled "Bush Battles the 'Wimp Factor'"
(Warner 1987). This same wimp label reemerged during the 2012 presidential election, again on the cover of *Newsweek*, only this time applied to
Republican presidential nominee Mitt Romney. In the article, the author
wrote that Romney is "risk averse," "annoying," and "whiny." Furthermore,
the article went on to say that "a Republican president sure of his manhood [like Reagan] has nothing to prove. . . . But a weenie Republican
[Romney]—look out" (Tomasky 2012). The "wimp" *Newsweek* headline
reprise is a clear sign of the relevance of masculinity in our politics and
especially to the office of the presidency.

The implications for women who run for office, and specifically the
presidency, are that "when women enter and act within the realm of leadership and governance, they do so within the ideological terms of masculine
norms. Therein lies the transformation of gender relations into gender
power relations" (Duerst-Lahti and Kelly 1995, 20). In other words, if the
rules of the game are masculine, the best way to compete is to replicate
masculinity. During the 2016 presidential race, this sort of conflict was
present in the discussions and media coverage of Hillary Clinton, the first
woman nominated to represent a major party in a presidential election. In
a postelection interview, Jennifer Palmieri, Clinton's director of commu-
nications, said,

I didn't appreciate at the beginning of the campaign how important models are for the person running and the public. So, the fact that we had never seen a woman do this before—this was a much bigger hindrance than I thought. And what I realized we had done to her is that we had made her a female facsimile of the qualities that we'd look for in a male president because there was no other way to think about the president. And I think that's why people thought she was inauthentic. And that's why you would hear people say things like "there is something about her I just don't like." (Palmieri 2018)

Here, Palmieri grapples with both the conceptual limitations for thinking about "the presidency" as confined to male norms and masculinity, and essentially their campaign's unconscious effort to force Clinton into this mold (see Goren 2018; Conroy 2018b). Although merely one anecdote from a long, drawn-out campaign, this is a powerful example of the gender hierarchy in American politics. To understand gender hierarchy and how it largely benefits men in American politics, it is important to conceptually divorce gender from sex. In this book, we consider how gender is internalized as gender personality, and argue that identification with a more masculine personality will have a positive influence on factors that contribute to progressive ambition: perception of qualification to run for higher office and greater recruitment contact.

Plan of the Book

We argue that politics and masculinity are congruent, and, thus, we should observe more precise variation in the candidate emergence process along gender differences than along sex differences in isolation. We expect that city councilmembers who possess more masculine personalities will be more likely to be recruited, perceive of themselves as qualified, and express progressive political ambition than will less masculine city councilmembers. This line of reasoning differs from studies that look at sex differences because it accepts and investigates that some women defy gender norms and break into politics. It is this defiance that we argue is explained by their gender personality. By including a measure of gender personality we can more fully grapple with women's progress in American politics, and consider whether this progress rests on masculine behaviors and attributes. We explore this possibility and discuss the potential ramifications.

In chapter 2 we review the origins of understanding women's underrepresentation in American politics and trace it back to the demand- and supply-side paradigm. Studies on demand-side factors consider the degree to which voters are willing to vote for women. Some research found that voters perceive women as less capable leaders than men, and thus have a preference for male candidates (Rosenwasser and Dean 1989; Butterfield and Powell 1981). However, other studies showed that there was less of an overt bias against women candidates when looking at actual vote choice—women win as often, or more often, than men (see Seltzer, Newman, and Leighton 1997; however, as we address in chapter 3, this observation is due in part to women's greater qualifications). This led to a focus on supply-side factors—if women win as often as men, why are women underrepresented? The speculation was that women are underrepresented because women do not run. Indeed, survey analyses find that women are less likely to run for political office and that this is due to a number of factors, including recruitment bias and a qualification gap—men are more likely to be asked, and more likely to see themselves as qualified, than women (see Lawless and Fox 2010 for a review). Given these findings, the current scholarship is focused squarely on understanding why women are less likely to be recruited, and why women are less likely to see themselves as qualified.

After we review the latest scholarship for understanding women's underrepresentation, we point to an additional, understudied, causal, psychological variable—gender personality. We define gender personality as an individual-level attribute that can be measured by an individual's self-identification with associated qualities, such as "confidence" and "decisiveness" for masculinity, and "devotion to others" and "warmth" for femininity. Men and women can possess varying degrees of femininity and masculinity, including both femininity and masculinity or neither. We operationalize gender personality using survey responses to the Personality Attributes Questionnaire, which was developed by psychologists Janet Spence and Robert Helmreich (1978). We discuss the development of the PAQ, as well as its limitations, in chapter 2.

In chapter 2, we also describe how we sampled and collected our data. Our survey instrument asked respondents about their experiences with political recruitment, perceptions of their qualifications for political office, and whether or not they have ambition to run for higher political office. We administered our survey to a nationally representative sample of around 3,500 city councilmembers from around the United States. Of those city councilmembers contacted, 679 responded.

In chapters 3, 4, and 5 we present our empirical assessment of the role of gender personality on our candidate emergence variables: perceptions of qualifications, recruitment experience, and progressive political ambition. Our theory points to masculinity as the nexus of internal (perception of qualification) and external (recruitment) routes of political ambition, and therefore more directly accounts for gender differences between and among women and men to explain candidate emergence and progressive ambition. Previous scholarship has identified the importance of these variables to the decision to run for office, yet has not directly investigated whether gender personality influences the degree to which individuals see themselves as qualified, or if it is correlated with their recruitment contact, to moderate their progressive political ambition. These chapters fill in these empirical gaps.

In chapter 3, we analyze city councilmembers' perception of their qualifications for higher office (Congress), and investigate whether these perceptions vary by gender personality. The qualification gap between men and women is well documented—women are less likely to believe they are qualified to run for political office, even though studies find women to be more qualified than their male counterparts when they do run (e.g., Fulton 2012). However, we expect that women (and men) who possess more masculine personalities will be less likely to succumb to qualification doubt. We argue that masculine personality should predict self-perceived qualifications, and that masculine men and women will perceive of themselves as more qualified for Congress than less masculine individuals. Our regression analysis finds that city councilmembers with more masculine personalities see themselves as more qualified to run for Congress. The qualification gap between men and women is reduced, but not erased, after accounting for the effects of gendered personality.

Additional analysis shows that those with a more masculine personality also report possession of more political skills—like fundraising or public speaking—which also affects qualification perceptions. We consider the consequences of this observed relationship and whether perceptions of qualification are a good indicator of candidate viability. We also discuss how femininity and perceptions of qualification might become better aligned to produce more gender diversity in successful candidate emergence. In other words, what elements of feminine identity are likely associated with perceptions of being unqualified, and what aspects of feminine identity could be emphasized by recruiters, for instance, as aligning with politics and government to increase gender diversity?

In chapter 4 we consider the role of recruitment in candidate emergence, and theorize that recruiters perceive potential candidates' gendered personality and are biased in favor of masculine individuals. Recruitment is important to the candidate emergence process. Typically, individuals do not consider running for public office until someone encourages them (Carroll and Sanbonmatsu 2013). Although past scholarship is mixed regarding differences in recruitment contact between men and women, this scholarship has yet to consider the explanatory value of individuals' gender personality. In this chapter, we review previous studies on candidate sex and experiences with recruitment. As we conduct our review, we highlight the implicitly gendered aspects of candidate recruitment, which are evident in past studies.

We place an emphasis on research related to gendered traits and ways in which Democrats and Republicans are similar and different in terms of gendered recruitment. In this manner, we draw out why masculinity should influence recruitment tendencies, why Democratic women may experience higher levels of recruitment contact than Republican women, and how gender helps to explain this phenomenon. Our regression analysis finds a positive relationship between masculinity and recruitment; people who possess more masculine personalities are rewarded—they are more likely to report being recruited regardless of their sex, with no clear ceiling of the effect for either men or women. Further, our analysis demonstrates that women's organizations also recruit masculine individuals (of both sexes), as do both political parties. We conclude that even as women grow more integrated into politics, masculine norms will remain intact if those women who are recruited are more masculine. In our discussion, we consider why primarily feminine women are less likely to be present in the eligibility pools where recruiters look for candidates, and propose new eligibility pools to be considered, which would increase gender diversity.

In chapter 5 we turn our attention to the indirect way in which masculinity affects progressive ambition. While Schlesinger (1966) effectively assumed a level of nascent ambition among all those well suited to run for political office, later research has shown that ambition is not constant (Carroll and Sanbonmatsu 2013), and in particular women are less ambitious than men, as traditionally measured (Lawless and Fox 2010). We expect that a masculine personality exerts a positive effect on qualifications and recruitment, which influences progressive political ambition, therefore finding an indirect role for gender personality in explaining progressive political ambition. In this chapter, we review the scholarship on political ambition that finds men to be more ambitious than women. We suggest that goal incongruity explains in part why feminine individuals have less ambition to follow political career paths. We then present our theory for an indirect role of gender on ambition, via perceptions of qualifications and recruitment, followed by analysis of this relationship. We show that including a measure of gender personality, in addition to perceptions of qualification and recruitment experience, leads to sex not exerting a significant effect on progressive political ambition. We discuss the importance of ambition as a product of qualifications and recruitment, and conclude that successful candidate emergence is the result of a confluence of factors, at the heart of which is masculinity.

In our concluding chapter, we briefly summarize our findings, and then consider the potential consequences of the political reality we uncover, beyond numerical representation of women in American political institutions. The political reality, according to our findings, is that women who successfully emerge to run for political office are more masculine than the women who do not. While this congruence predicts their successful navigation of the masculine terrain of American politics, what might our politics be losing, given this gender personality imbalance? For example, what are the public policy consequences of a political culture that privileges masculinity and disparages, excludes, or undervalues femininity? We also consider how media and the nature of political campaigns might be contributing to this gender hierarchy, where masculinity enables political advantages. Finally, we conclude with how our work can and should be extended to incorporate theories for whether race, sexuality, and other intersecting identities may affect the relationships our analysis reveals. As we note in chapter 2, our city council sample is 88 percent white, which therefore limits our analysis with respect to drawing conclusions about the intersection of race and gender personality. Finally, we suggest possible means of dismantling the masculine norms in American politics, such as structural changes to our political institutions and an evolution of social norms that contribute to the gendered hierarchy in politics.

TWO

The Underrepresentation of Women

Past Discoveries and New Directions

Despite steady progress over time, women are still underrepresented in American politics at all levels of government. Although it varies by state, on average women make up 28.9 percent of state legislatures (Center for American Women in Politics 2019). Following the 2018 election cycle, only 10 out of 50 governors are women and 20 states have *never* had a woman as their governor. In the U.S. Congress, women hold 23.7 percent of congressional seats, up from 19.6 percent before the 2018 election cycle; following the 1998 elections, women made up just 12 percent of Congress. Thus, modest progress has been made over the last 20 years, even though, overall, women hold a meager share of elected positions at these levels of government (see fig. 2.1).

Although there has been modest progress, women should be gaining more ground given their progress in other professional fields. Moreover, women now outnumber men at the polls, showcasing their willingness to participate in the political process (Seltzer, Newman, and Leighton 1997). However, barriers still exist that prevent women from attaining positions of power where they can wield influence. This disparity in representation is important to understand for a number of reasons. In particular, as Carroll and Sanbonmatsu (2013, 2) note, "the persistent gender imbalance in office holding raises questions about democratic legitimacy, the inclusivity of American politics, and the quality of political representation." Therefore, we need to ask more questions and develop better solutions to remedy this

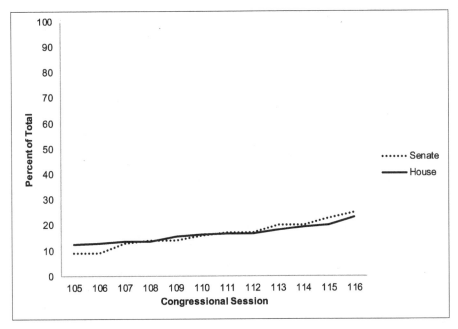

Fig. 2.1. Indirect Model of Masculine Personality and Progressive Ambition
(Data from the Center for American Women and Politics, 2019.)

inequality. In this chapter, we will review previous scholarship focused on the underrepresentation of women in politics in the United States, while drawing out the implicit connections between this work and our variable of interest: internalized gender personality.

Why do women still trail behind men in holding elected office? One possibility is that voters are biased against women. This "demand-side" explanation of women's underrepresentation places the onus on those who go to the polls and select candidates. Most of these studies from the 1980s and 1990s found that voters perceive women as less capable leaders than men, and thus had a preference for male candidates (Huddy and Terkildsen 1993; Rosenwasser and Dean 1989). However, there is less of an overt bias against women candidates when looking at actual vote choice—women win as often as men (Herrnson, Lay, and Stokes 2003; Lawless and Pearson 2008). However, Fulton (2012) shows this may be due to women's greater qualifications; in other words, women do better than men when they run because, on average, the women who decide to run have more experience than the men who run (see also Branton et al. 2018; Barnes, Branton, and Cassese 2017; Anzia and Berry 2011; O'Brien and Rickne 2016; Pearson and McGhee 2013). Experimen-

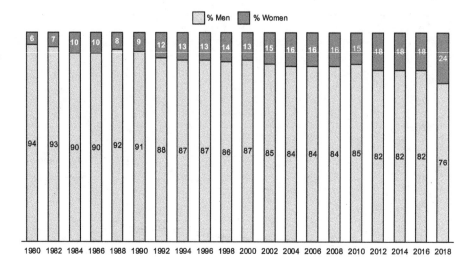

Fig. 2.2. U.S. House Primary Candidates, 1980–2018
(Data from Danielle Thomsen, 2018, "Women Are Less Than a Quarter of All House Candidates This Year, but That's Still Record Breaking." http://cawp.rutgers.edu/footnotes/women-are-less-quarter-all-us-house-candidates-year-thats-record-breaking)

tal studies using conjoint designs, where experience is similar for male and female candidates, offer mixed findings (Teele, Kalla, and Rosenbluth 2018; Ono and Burden 2018). Regardless, these mixed and minimal indications that voters express overt bias against women have led to a focus on supply-side factors, or the lack of supply of women candidates. In short, if women win as often as men, their underrepresentation may be due to their reluctance to run. Straightforward analysis does find that women are less likely to run for political office; even in the new "Year of the Woman," as 2018 was called, women still lagged behind men (fig. 2.2).

While numerous political, structural, and psychological sources contribute to the gap in men and women running for office, two clear sources are recruitment bias and a qualification gap—men are more likely to be asked to run, and they are more likely to see themselves as qualified to run (e.g., Lawless and Fox 2010). Given these findings, new scholarship is focused on factors that influence recruitment efforts and individuals' perception that they are qualified to run.

The study of the underrepresentation of women in politics largely looks at differences between men and women (e.g., perceptions of qualification among men versus women, or differences in recruitment contact between men and women). While sex is the analytical focus of these studies, they clearly point to the importance of gender—masculinity and femininity—to explain women's underrepresentation. Our goal is to broaden the analytical framework from sex to include gender, both in terms of input and output. In particular, we conceptualize an internalized form of gender—gender personality. We argue that a masculine personality gives candidates an edge in the candidate emergence process, and a by-product is not just an underrepresentation of women but also of femininity in our political institutions.

After we review the latest scholarship for understanding women's underrepresentation, we point to an additional and understudied causal variable—gender personality. We define gender personality as an individual-level attribute that can be measured by an individual's self-identification with associated qualities, such as "confidence" and "aggression" for a masculine personality and "devotion to others" and "warmth" for a feminine personality. Men and women can possess varying degrees of feminine and masculine personality, including both feminine and masculine or neither. We measure masculinity and femininity as distinct sets of personality traits. We operationalize gender personality with the Personality Attributes Questionnaire instrument, developed by psychologists Janet Spence and Robert Helmreich (Spence and Helmreich 1978). We discuss the development of the PAQ, as well as its limitations, in this chapter.

This chapter will also explain how we sampled and collected our data. Our survey instrument asked sitting city councilmembers, so those who have already exhibited some level of political ambition, about their experiences with political recruitment, perceptions of their qualifications for Congress, and whether or not they have ambitions to run for higher political office. The survey also includes the PAQ and was administered to about 3,500 city councilmembers. Members were selected by compiling a list of cities with over 10,000 residents. From this list, we randomly selected 590 cities from which to draw our respondents. This nested sampling design cast a wide net to ensure representativeness and generalizability. Of city councilmembers contacted, 679 responded.[1] After an explanation of our research design, sample, and survey instrument, we briefly describe our expectations and hypotheses, which we assess in chapters 3, 4, and 5.

---

1. Our response rate is 23%, roughly equivalent to, or better than, other similar surveys. For example, a recent study by Teele, Kalla, and Rosenbluth (2018) of elected officials reports a response rate of 9% and explains that "some recent surveys of public officials in the United States use both email- and mail-based solicitations to achieve response rates closer to 19% making our response rate of 9% an achievement" (530). Some submitted surveys were incomplete or missing responses to one or more key variables. Item nonresponse is dealt with through listwise deletion.

Demand: Gender Stereotypes and the Underrepresentation of Women in Government

Demand-side barriers to women's representation refer to external factors, such as the public's perception of female candidates and whether voters are willing to support women who run for office. In a straightforward assessment of "demand," Gallup has been asking individuals, "If your party nominated a woman for president, would you vote for her if she were qualified for the job?" In 1937, 33 percent indicated that they would vote for a woman; by 2012, that number had shot up to 95 percent; in 2015 there was a slight drop (table 2.1).

In 2005, support for a woman president dropped to 86 percent. This decline in support may expose an underlying cause for reservations toward women in political leadership positions, particularly the office of president. After the September 11, 2001 terrorist attack, the 2004 presidential candidates focused much of their campaigning efforts on issues of national security, terrorism, and war. In 2002, Gallup polls found almost half of those sampled indicated that war and terrorism was the most important issue facing the country, compared to around 10 percent expressing this sentiment before the attack (Lawless 2004). As Lawless (2004, 480) notes, "A clear bias favoring male candidates and elected officials accompanies the war on terror." She continues, "Citizens prefer men's leadership traits and characteristics, deem men more competent at legislating around issues of national security and military crises, and contend that men are superior to women at addressing the new obstacles generated by the events of September 11, 2001" (480). Indeed, Lawless found that two-thirds of survey respondents did not believe men and women were equally suited to deal with military crises. Of the two-thirds, 95 percent stated that men are better able than women to deal with military affairs. Therefore, it is very likely that decline in support for a woman president in 2005 was due to the prominence of terrorism and national security and the belief that women are less suited to handle these issues. The crux of the belief that women are less suited to deal with issues like terrorism and national security is rooted in women's

TABLE 2.1. Public Support for a Female President

Year	1937	1948	1958	1978	1999	2005	2012	2015	2019
"yes" (%)	33	48	54	76	92	86	95	92	94

Source: Gallup 2019.

Note: Gallup poll question: "If your party nominated a generally well-qualified person for president who happened to be a woman, would you vote for that person?"

association with femininity, which stems from gender stereotypes. Gender stereotypes are stereotypes about men and women and largely assume men are masculine and women are feminine.

Gender stereotypes about women are present in abstract evaluations of hypothetical political candidates (Sanbonmatsu 2002; Sanbonmatsu and Dolan 2009; Dolan 2010; Dolan and Lynch 2014). Hypothetical female candidates are seen as possessing feminine qualities, such as compassion, and having expertise on feminine issues, such as education and health care, whereas hypothetical male candidates are seen as possessing masculine qualities, such as assertiveness, and having expertise on masculine issues, such as terrorism (Huddy and Terkildsen 1993; Kahn 1996; Fox and Oxley 2003; Lawless 2004; Fridkin and Kenney 2009; Dolan 2010, 2014). These observations that gender stereotypes pervade politics are mostly drawn from data collected from survey responses or laboratory settings, where respondents are asked whether they perceive that men and women have distinct policy expertise and possess distinct traits. Although much of this scholarship does not assess the effects of gender stereotypes on actual vote choice, the presumption is that gender stereotypes hurt women who run because the feminine gender is incongruent with political leadership.

As past scholarship has found, voters value masculine traits more than feminine traits in their political leaders (Niven 1998; Gordon and Miller 2003; Heith 2003; Lawless 2004; Offerman and Coates 2018), likely due to the perception that political leadership necessitates more masculine qualities to be done effectively (Koenig et al. 2011). This masculine advantage is oftentimes embraced by women, and for good reason: experiments demonstrate that when women emphasize more masculine characteristics in their campaign materials they have an advantage over men who do not (Bauer 2018a; see also Bauer 2018b). Additionally, Bystrom et al. (2004) show that women are less likely to feature their families in political advertising, possibly illustrative of avoiding contexts that inhibit associations with masculinity (see also Stalsburg and Kleinberg 2015).

The existence of stereotypes about traits and issue expertise for men and women in politics has led to scholarship interested in the degree to which these stereotypes are electorally consequential (Hayes 2011; Dolan and Lynch 2014; Hayes and Lawless 2016), for whom (Dolan 2010; Bauer 2015a), and in what political context (Sanbonmatsu 2002; Lawless 2004; Dolan 2004; Falk and Kenski 2006; Holman, Merolla, and Zechmeister 2016). Although results are mixed, most agree that while voters hold stereotypical views about men and women in politics, when it comes down to vote choice, party identification explains more of their decision (Hayes

2011; Dolan and Lynch 2014). However, in particular contexts, gender is more relevant. For example, when the issue of terrorism is salient (Holman, Merolla, and Zechmeister 2016; Falk and Kenski 2006), when respondents are primed to consider candidate sex (Sanbonmatsu and Dolan 2009; Sanbonmatsu 2002), for less attentive voters (Bauer 2015b), or for gender essentialists (Swigger and Meyer 2018), gender stereotypes are at least partially influential.

However, taking a slightly different approach to gender stereotypes in evaluations of men and women, Schneider and Bos (2014) suggest that female politicians may represent a sub*type*, as opposed to a sub*group* of women; a subgroup would expect women running for office to be perceived in terms of stereotypes about women, but a subtype would not expect similarities between perceptions of these two groups. A subtype is "a new stereotypical category, created when perceivers encounter a group that deviates from a larger stereotype category" (249). Schneider and Bos (2014) argue that the perceptions of women who run for political office are distinct from perceptions of women in general, and that the traditional model for assessing whether female politicians are seen as holding traditional feminine traits does not allow for this subtype to emerge.

To test whether female politicians are a subtype of women the authors first asked participants to describe "male professionals," "female professionals," "male politicians," "female politicians," "politicians," "men," and "women" (Schneider and Bos 2014). From these descriptions, they created a list of adjectives, and then asked a different group of participants to indicate which adjectives that they thought "people in general" would use to describe the particular groups listed. What they confirmed is that male politicians are a subgroup of men; those traits most commonly selected to describe male politicians, such as leader, competitive, aggressive, and driven, were also used to describe men in general. Yet there was much less overlap between the adjectives selected to describe women and female politicians. Caring, motherly, feminine, and emotional were the most common selected traits to describe women. However, for female politicians, these traits were not widely agreed upon. The authors conclude that there is not much agreement on descriptions of female politicians, and that "female politicians are defined more by their deficits than their strengths" (Schneider and Bos 2014, 260). This research suggests that although stereotypes about women may not be salient when individuals are thinking about women running for political office, association with womanhood does not give female candidates an advantage in the abstract.

Inherent in this body of work is the recognition that associations with femininity are typically costly, and many analyses bear this out. However, acknowledging that the possession of gender stereotypes by potential voters cannot fully account for women's underrepresentation, scholars have turned to supply-side factors that influence women's entrance into politics. Much of the scholarship on this topic has focused on recruitment bias and perceptions of qualification; however, studies of political opportunity consider structural and situational sources of women's lack of interest, as well (e.g., Silberman 2015; Carroll and Sanbonmatsu 2013).

Supply: Why Are Women Less Likely to Run?

Recruitment Bias

One reason that women may not be as eager as men to run for office is because women are less likely to be encouraged to run. Encouragement can come in the form of a local party official reaching out to someone in the community to run for a seat, or from a personal friend or family member. In this sense, recruitment influences the supply of candidates. At the same time, an individual's likelihood of being recruited may still be moderated by recruiters' external perceptions of femininity or masculinity. Therefore, the factors we reviewed that explain demand (gender and leadership stereotypes) are also relevant to recruitment.

Recruitment is especially consequential for inexperienced individuals, women, and men and women of color. As Moncrief, Squire, and Jewell (2001) find, only one-third of first-time candidates make the decision to run on their own; the other two-thirds of candidates make the decision to run for office after encouragement, typically from party officials and representatives. Among women, 24 percent reported encouragement as the most important factor in their decision to run, compared to just 15 percent of men (Sanbonmatsu, Carroll, and Walsh 2009). Indeed, Karpowitz, Monson, and Preece (2017) find that messages from party leaders to Republican women stoke their interest in running for office, demonstrating the importance of recruitment contact and encouragement. Last, Juenke and Shah (2016) suggest that the underrecruitment of people of color contributes to their underrepresentation in elected office.

The bulwark of studies on recruitment finds that men are more likely to say they were recruited to run than women (Carroll 1994; Lawless and Fox 2010; Fox and Lawless 2014; Kirkpatrick 1974; Moncrief, Squire, and Jewell 2001; Norris and Lovenduski 1995; Sanbonmatsu 2006; Welch 1978;

Windett 2014; Sweet-Cushman 2018). There is some evidence that this is due to recruitment practices. For instance, recruiters' personal networks are important for identifying possible candidates; however, personal networks are homogenous, therefore men recruit other men, perpetuating inequalities in representation (Sanbonmatsu 2006). Recruiter's own bias also influences their contacts. For example, using an experimental design, Doherty, Dowling, and Miller (2019) assess how local party chairs' own personal opinions about candidate viability come into play and might influence recruitment tendencies. Although the authors find local party chairs view female candidates as just as likely to win support of their party's base as male candidates, local party chairs view Black and Latino candidates (similarly for men and women) as less likely to win than white candidates. In sum, the personal bias of recruiters has consequences for recruitment contact, whether or not that bias is deliberate.

Outside of personal networks, recruiters draw from a pool of "eligible" candidates with traditional professional experiences in business, law, or in state and local politics. As Crowder-Meyer (2013) shows, when parties recruit from these traditional pools, the process disadvantages women because women are less likely to be present in these eligibility pools. Moreover, the women in these traditional pools are more similar to men than to women who are not in these pools (Crowder-Meyer 2018). Thus, the recruitment of "eligible" women, who come from occupations traditionally connected to political networking, may be more similar to men in terms of gender personality.

Others have looked at how the recruitment process might be better suited to men. For example, Butler and Preece (2016) find that men are more receptive than women to the approach that recruiters typically take. Additionally, recruitment appeals that describe running for office as a community-building endeavor actually close the political ambition gap (Pate and Fox 2018). Focusing on the contextual nature of elections and recruitment deepens our understanding of the observed supply variation by sex. But implicit in these previous analyses is evidence of a more explicit role for internalized gender personality to explain candidate recruitment variation.

Self-Perceived Qualifications

In addition to recruitment bias contributing to the scant supply of women running for office, individuals' self-perceived qualification influence their interest in running for political office. Self-perceived qualification is an individual's belief that he or she is qualified to run for political office. When asked if individuals see themselves as qualified to run for political office, men are more likely to express the belief that they are qualified, while women are much less likely. As Lawless and Fox (2010, 166) show, from a pool of objectively qualified individuals, 60 percent of men expressed that they thought they were "qualified" or "very qualified" compared to just 39 percent of women—a whopping 21-point gap.

Women's lower levels of self-perceived qualifications are certainly tied to socialization (Thomas 2005; Fox and Lawless 2014). For example, from childhood and onward, young boys are encouraged to be competitive, while young girls are not; boys are exposed to political discussion more than girls; boys are more encouraged than girls to consider political careers (e.g., Lawless and Fox 2015). Moreover, women are socialized to prioritize home and family, which leads women with political ambitions to delay entry into politics, and therefore a political career (Elder 2004; Lawless and Fox 2010; Fox and Lawless 2014; Sapiro 1981). Taken together, there is strong evidence pointing to political socialization as contributing to women's diminished perception that they are qualified to run for political office.

But the perception among most women that they are not qualified is also linked to the perception of political office as necessitating masculine skills or engaging in masculine behaviors. For example, Preece and Stoddard (2015) show that women are more averse to running for political office if competition is an assumed norm of politics. Kanthak and Woon (2015) also find women to be election averse due to the anticipation of competition. Therefore, women are responsive to the electoral environment and institutional context, which we argue are gendered. Pate and Fox (2018) find additional evidence that women (and men) make connections between the electoral environment and their own skills and goals. In their study, when messages about running for political office emphasize community building, women demonstrate higher levels of ambition than men. This coincides with scholarship that shows women are more likely to have communal career goals, but perceive of political office as incongruent with those goals, explaining their reluctance (Schneider et al. 2016).

The vast body of literature on candidate emergence and women's underrepresentation convincingly implicates gender, yet direct measurement of both the gendered terrain and internalized gender personality differences, and how the two do and do not interact, is limited. While there are a number of ways to address this gap in the literature, we take a personality-based approach, where we directly measure individuals' identification with various masculine and feminine attributes, and assess whether gender personality contributes to differences in recruitment, qualification, and progressive ambition.

Gender Personality and Women's Underrepresentation in Politics

Why study personality? Personality has been described as "the entire mental organization of a human being at any stage of his development. It embraces every phase of human character: intellect, temperament, skill, morality, and every attitude that has been built up in the course of one's life" (Warren and Carmichael 1930, 333). In particular, *traits* describe the typical manner or style of an individual's behavior (Ebstein, Benjamin, and Belmaker 2003), and are enduring or chronic characteristics (Caprara et al. 2006).

Political psychologists have used surveys to assess the relationship between various political attitudes and behaviors and individuals' personality on five dimensions (the Big Five)—Openness, Conscientiousness, Extraversion, Agreeableness, and Neuroticism. For example, personality predicts attitudes like party identification (Carney et al. 2008; Gerber et al. 2010, 2012; Mondak 2010), and behaviors like political discussion (Hibbing, Ritchie, and Anderson 2011) and persuadability (Gerber et al. 2013). Indeed, there is no shortage of studies that find a relationship between various personality traits and political phenomena. Recent scholarship has even investigated a link between the Big Five and nascent and progressive political ambition (Dynes, Hassell, and Miles 2019).

Although political science has embraced personality studies, and indeed was an early adopter of such studies (e.g., Lasswell 1930; Lane 1962), the incorporation of gender personality has been slow. However, there is good reason to expect gender personality to moderate political attitudes and behaviors. For example, McDermott (2016) shows that gender personality predicts partisan identification, vote choice, political knowledge, interest, and attitudes about sex roles in social and political contexts; the more strongly an individual identifies with feminine personality traits, the more strongly they identify with the Democratic Party, and the more strongly they identify with a masculine personality the more strongly they identify as Republican.

Beyond mass-level attitudes and behaviors, there is still ample ground to cover, assessing the influence of gender personality on political phenomena. We argue that gender personality should help explain candidate emergence among sitting city councilmembers; we expect gender personality influences perception that they are qualified to run for Congress, their experiences with recruitment, and therefore their progressive political ambition.

The Personal Attributes Questionnaire

Our primary interest is in gender personality as an antecedent to political ambition, by way of self-perceived qualification and recruitment contact. In particular, we focus on masculinity as a personality attribute. Our definition of masculinity is drawn from the social psychology literature on gender and studies of gender personality traits (see chapter 1 for more on this). Masculinity and femininity are dimensions of gender personality. The facets of these trait dimensions are linked to the social expectations of men and women, respectively (see Schneider and Bos 2019). These traits, like other dimensions of personality, are generally stable over time, though they can shift over long periods (Donnelly and Twenge 2012). To measure gender personality, we use the Personal Attributes Questionnaire (Spence, Helmreich, and Stapp, 1975).

Development and Measurement of the PAQ

The Personal Attributes Questionnaire is a common measure of masculinity and femininity in social psychology, with separate scales for each on a spectrum from least to most masculine and feminine, respectively (Spence, Helmreich, and Stapp 1975). To develop the PAQ, Janet Spence and her colleagues (Spence, Helmreich, and Stapp 1975; Spence and Helmreich 1978) recruited undergraduates to categorize a set of personality traits as desirable in men, desirable in women, more common in men, and more common in women. They also asked participants to rate themselves on the traits. The self-ratings created an average score for each sex in the participant pool for each trait. The researchers examined the trends in the results, looking for personality traits that were overall rated as more common in men than in women and vice versa. These were the set of traits that corresponded to gender stereotypes, or that are particularly gendered. They then selected traits that were rated as desirable for both sexes.

From the analysis of these data, Spence and her colleagues developed the scales that capture three dimensions of gendered traits. The masculinity scale, or M scale, contains traits rated by the undergraduates as desirable for both sexes but more common in men (like "self-confident"). The femininity scale, or F scale, included traits desirable for men and women but more common in women (like "warm"). A third set of traits was also created as a bipolar masculinity-femininity scale (M-F scale), in which the traits were split between those rated as desirable and common for men but not women (like "aggressive") and those more desirable and more common in women than men (like "cries easily"). This third subscale, unlike the other two scales, is a bipolar, instead of a unidimensional, measure. This third scale also has an unclear connection to our outcomes of interest. Therefore, we rely on only the M and F subscales for our analysis and will focus only on these portions of the PAQ for the remainder of our analysis.

The traits on the masculine scale, in addition to being more stereotypically prevalent in men and positively connoted for men, are also conceptually agentic traits. Each trait relates to a way in which an individual interacts with the world as an individual, with independence and self-assertion (Spence and Helmreich 1978). The traits on the femininity scale all revolve around the concept of communality, and are positive for interpersonal interactions and relationship building. We discuss why the conceptual and empirical unidimensionality of the PAQ is particularly suited to our study of progressive political ambition.

The masculinity scale is operationalized as a summative index capturing respondent identification with the eight masculine attributes from the PAQ. The femininity scale is operationalized as an index capturing respondent identification with eight feminine attributes (table 2.2). For each question, respondents were asked about what level of a single attribute they most identify with on a scale from 1 to 5 (recoded to 0 through 4). For instance, one item runs between "not at all competitive" and "very competitive," where "not at all competitive" would be coded as a 0 and "very competitive" is coded as a 4.

The index for respondent masculinity was calculated by summing across the eight items for the masculine scale. This resulted in an overall index score, with a potential score from 0 (all attributes on the extreme

TABLE 2.2. Masculine and Feminine Items from the Personal Attributes Questionnaire

Masculine (Agentic) Traits	Feminine (Communality) Traits
Independent	Emotional
Active	Devotes self to others
Competitive	Gentle
Can make decisions easily	Helpful to others
Doesn't give up easily	Kind
Self-confident	Aware of the feelings of others
Feels superior	Understanding of others
Stands up well under pressure	Warm in relations with others

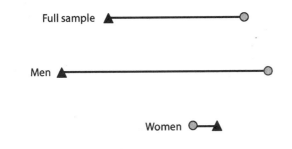

Fig. 2.3. Average Masculinity and Femininity Scale Scores for Our Sample of City Councilmembers, Broken Down by Sex
(*Note:* Femininity and Masculinity scores are calculated from responses to the Personality Attributes Questionnaire.)

nonmasculine end, such as "not at all competitive") to 32 (all attributes on the extreme masculine end, such as "very competitive"). The same procedure was used to calculate a score on the femininity scale. Index scores for masculinity ranged from 4 to 32, with a mean of 24.24 (SD = 3.74; Mdn = 24). The femininity scale ranged from 9 to 32, with a mean of 23.56 (SD = 3.82, Mdn = 24). Among our sample, men and women did not exhibit significantly different scores on the masculinity scale (M_{men} = 24.36, SD = 3.73; M_{women} = 23.98, SD = 3.78; t = –1.17, p > .10). Men and women did exhibit differences in identification with femininity. Women had a higher mean femininity score of 24.10 (SD = 3.72), and men had a lower mean femininity score of 23.32 (SD = 3.83), which is a small difference substantively but is statistically significant (t = 2.37, p = .02) (see figure 2.3).

Figure 2.4 presents the average masculine and feminine personality scores by respondent sex and party affiliation. Democratic women have the highest femininity average (24.02). Both Democratic men and Republican women have the same average femininity score (23.79). Republican men have the widest difference in their identification with femininity and masculinity ($M_{masculinity}$ = 24.32, $M_{femininity}$ = 22.97, $M_{difference}$ = 1.35; t = 3.65, p < .05); Democratic women on average are similarly masculine and feminine, suggesting a more androgynous gender personality ($M_{masculinity}$ = 24.05, $M_{femininity}$ = 24.04, $M_{difference}$ = 0.01; t = .02, p > .10).

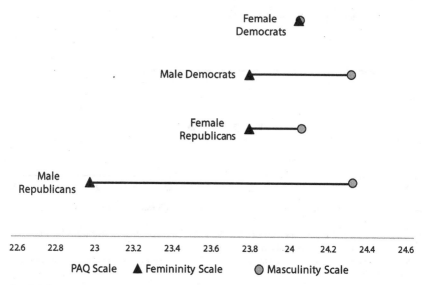

PAQ Scale   ▲ Femininity Scale   ◉ Masculinity Scale

Fig. 2.4. Average Masculine and Feminine Personality Scores for Men and Women Democrats and Republicans

(Note: Femininity and Masculinity scores are calculated from responses to the Personality Attributes Questionnaire.)

Reliability and Validity of the PAQ: Previous Studies and Comparison to the BSRI

There have been a number of tests of the psychometric properties of the PAQ, to assess its reliability and validity as a construct. Ward et al. (2006) tested the full PAQ, including the M-F scale, and found that each sub-scale (M scale, F scale, and M-F scale) loaded onto a separate factor, and therefore found the PAQ to be reliable. However, "emotional" (feminine), "active" (masculine), and "decisive" (masculine) traits showed weak factor loadings. This is similar to the results in our factor analysis, which we review below. Although Ward et al. (2006) and others (e.g., Curran and Warber 2011) are critical of the PAQ given some weak factor loadings, our assessment is that this measure is satisfactory for our purposes, and we present factor analysis below that will support our decision to rely on the PAQ measure for this study. However, we do not use the M-F portion of the scale. We conclude that the unidimensional structure of the masculinity and femininity PAQ subscales provides the most straightforward and valid measurement of the concepts we are interested in.

Masculinity and femininity as dimensions of a gender personality are theoretically stable constructs within an individual, but there have been changes at the population level over time (Spence and Buckner 2000; Twenge 1997). Therefore, another important consideration of the validity of the PAQ as an instrument is its stability over time. There is not much existing literature to directly address this point empirically, but there is some indication that the PAQ does lead to stable results within individuals. For instance, Yoder et al. (1982) found high reliability across a 2.5 month period, and Twenge (1997) finds that the levels of masculinity and femininity are stable in different samples in a short period; however, Twenge does find that identification with femininity overall has gone down over time, between the 1970s and 1990s, although the change is slight. This suggests that, within individuals, the construct is stable, but rates vary by generation. In Spence and Buckner's (2000) analysis of the PAQ 25 years after its development, they explain that as social and cultural standards for men and women have changed, so have their adoption of different traits stereotypically linked to men and women. For instance, as women enter the workforce and gain a self-conception consistent with a life in the public sphere, they also adopt more agentic (or masculine) personality traits. Once adopted, however, there is little reason to think these women would later abandon these traits. Although this finding offers evidence that possession of feminine and masculine gender stereotypes is no longer unique to men and women, respectively, we are confident in the validity and reliability of the PAQ as a measure of gender personality in individuals. Other scales of personality likewise show stability over time, lending more confidence that the PAQ should be stable through one's lifetime (see McDermott 2016 for a review).

In our pursuit of an appropriate measure for gender personality as a causal factor on candidate emergence, we found two primary options within the social psychology literature: the Bem Sex Role Inventory (BSRI), developed by Sandra Bem (1993), and the PAQ. Both of these instruments conceptualize gender personality from a list of unique feminine and masculine attributes. One key difference between the two measures is that the PAQ is narrower in the selection of facets that measure masculinity and femininity, focusing on instrumentality for masculinity and expressiveness for femininity. For instance, agentic facets of personality include one's dominance in the world, assertiveness, confidence, and competitiveness. Facets of expressiveness are building and sustaining relationships with others, and being helpful, kind, and warm. The BSRI, on the other hand, incorporates a broader set of masculine and feminine attributes. The BSRI measures masculinity and femininity with a 60-item battery, although it was later pared down to 30 questions for a short-form version (Bem 1981). Both the BSRI and PAQ have been shown to be internally consistent, with alpha coefficients of at least .70 and in some cases up to .90 (Choi 2004); some studies show somewhat higher internal consistency for the BSRI than the PAQ, which is thought to be related to the more complicated calculation of the PAQ scale.

The PAQ and BSRI are fairly similar in their general construction, but there are differences between these two indexes that led us to use the PAQ over the BSRI to measure gendered personality. One key difference between the scales is the factor structure and loadings of individual traits on the BSRI. For the long-form BSRI, factor analyses suggested that terms deemed either masculine or feminine loaded on more than one factor (Choi, Fuqua, and Newman 2009). Also, some traits that fit poorly were still included (Choi and Fuqua 2003; Choi, Fuqua, and Newman 2009; Colley et al. 2009). Even with the short form, analyses have found a better fit with a three-factor solution than with two factors (Colley et al. 2009).

Beyond measurement, conceptual criticism on the BSRI also abounds. For example, Choi and colleagues (2009) found that there were two distinct aspects of masculinity in the BSRI—personal and social masculinity. The PAQ has also faced a number of criticisms and had low factor loadings of some traits, but overall the facets are more likely to fit a clear two-factor solution based around agentic traits for masculinity and communal traits for femininity (Twenge 1997; Choi 2004; Spence and Helmreich 1978; Ward et al. 2006; Yoder et al. 1982).

The PAQ has the advantage of homing in on traits that are all tied to particular aspects of masculinity and femininity, while the BSRI lacks this focus, especially in the original long form. In creating the BSRI, Sandra Bem (1993) sought all attributes related to masculinity and femininity, seeking a broad swath of terms related to gender schemas. Janet Spence, on the other hand, sought a scale that targeted particular dimensions of masculinity and femininity, focused around instrumentality and expressivity (Eagly and Wood 2017). Spence (2011) notes that a narrower definition of gendered personality increases its utility in predicting outcomes in attitudes and behavior related to the PAQ. The BSRI short form was narrowed based on factor loadings rather than conceptual relations, and therefore retains a broader set of traits, as well as a multidimensional concept. McDermott (2016) argued in favor of the BSRI over the PAQ in her study of the effects of masculinity and femininity on political attitudes, ideology, and participation among a general population sample, because the BSRI is a better fit for her theory. In particular, she separates the respondents into sex types based on Bem's (1993) typology and research on androgyny. In our work, the focus is more narrowly focused on the decision to run for political office as well as lacking the focus on androgyny, so the PAQ is preferred.

The concept of instrumentality—a defining characteristic of masculinity in the PAQ—is particularly useful for predicting entry into a political career. Confidence, ambition, and decisiveness are three indicators of masculinity that fit within the notion of an ideal politician (e.g., Schneider and Bos 2014). The masculinity scale of the PAQ overlaps with characteristics generally thought to be associated with a prototypically good politician, such as confidence, competitiveness, and independence. The PAQ is not, however, equivalent to a measure of strong political leadership skills. For instance, a recent study of the various gendered and nongendered traits that are associated with politicians, as well as with specifically male and female politicians, found that a number of the most popular traits were those that are also masculine, although some of the most common traits were not specifically gendered in nature (Schneider and Bos 2014). Respondents associated the traits "competitive," "active," and "driven" with politicians, and "confident" with male politicians. All of these traits are included in the PAQ to measure masculinity. Other nonmasculine traits used to describe politicians included intelligence and competence, motivation, and charisma (Schneider and Bos 2014). Therefore, masculine traits compose a part of what people see as general leadership skills, but masculinity as measured by the PAQ is not synonymous with political leadership.

Descriptive Results and Factor Analysis of the PAQ for City Councilmembers

Once we collected our data, we conducted additional analyses to be confident that our measure of gender personality was sufficiently valid for use as our primary predictor. First, we report descriptive statistics for gender personality and compare them to existing studies of this measure. The average score on the PAQ masculinity scale for our sample of city councilmembers was higher than a sample of university students (Keener, Strough, and Didonato 2012) and a sample of business managers (Vinnicombe and Singh 2002). Among university students, the mean masculine scale for men/women was 21.9/19.9 (for our sample the mean masculinity scale was 24.4/24). We also compare our sample to a more similar sample of business managers. For that sample, mean masculine scales were much closer to our sample. The average masculine scale score of women in the sample of business managers was 23.1 and 23.5 for men. Although this demonstrates that masculine personality varies across population differences, there is substantial variation in the levels of masculinity among individuals in our sample, and thus we expect to observe differences in our variables of interest along this dimension. Moreover, for all three samples compared, standard deviations were similar.

To further demonstrate the validity of the PAQ for our sample we performed an exploratory factor analysis and present the full findings below (table 2.3). The observed masculinity and femininity scales for our sample show an acceptable level of reliability, with a Cronbach's alpha of .73 for the masculine scale and .77 for the feminine scale for the analysis of all respondents, similar to other data on the PAQ (see Choi 2004). Table 2.3

TABLE 2.3. Factor Analysis with a Rotated Promax Solution for Masculinity and Femininity Scales of the PAQ, by Gender

PAQ Subscales	All Respondents		Men Only		Women Only	
	Feminine	Masculine	Feminine	Masculine	Feminine	Masculine
Feminine (F Scale)						
Emotional	.28	–.14	.32	–.10	.20	–.27
Devotes Self Completely	**.50**	.09	**.50**	.14	**.46**	.01
Gentle	**.44**	–.18	**.44**	–.18	**.47**	–.2
Helpful	**.56**	.14	**.58**	.09	**.56**	.21
Kind	**.66**	.00	**.68**	–.01	**.66**	.00
Aware of Feelings	**.68**	–.07	**.67**	–.07	**.70**	–.07
Understanding	**.73**	.02	**.72**	.02	**.76**	.00
Warm	**.59**	.01	**.61**	.03	**.51**	–.03
Masculine (M Scale)						
Independent	–.03	.39	–.07	**.47**	.02	.27
Active	.04	**.46**	.02	**.54**	–.01	.39
Competitive	–.03	**.48**	.04	**.41**	–.09	**.57**
Makes Decisions Easily	–.16	**.59**	–.17	**.56**	–.10	**.62**
Never Gives Up Easily	.12	**.47**	.13	**.41**	.14	**.57**
Self-Confident	–.03	**.74**	.00	**.73**	–.04	**.75**
Feels Superior	–.10	.37	–.09	.38	–.07	.36
Stands Up Well Under Pressure	.05	**.64**	.01	**.67**	.15	**.59**
Sample Size	529		436		193	
Eigenvalue	3.91	2.32	4.11	2.20	3.68	2.58
Percent Explained	24.43%	14.48%	25.67%	13.77%	23.03%	16.15%
Chronbach's Alpha	.77	.73	.78	.74	.75	.73

Note: Masculine Scale is identified by the masculine pole; the Feminine Scale is identified by the feminine pole. Loadings above .4 are indicated in bold.

shows a principal axis factor analysis with promax rotation. We tested multiple other rotations for these analyses and found the promax results to fit the best for these data. Orthogonal, oblique, and varimax rotations were similar, but less coherent. Also, since the subscales and individual questions on the PAQ do correlate with one another, the assumptions of the promax solution best fit the data. The number of factors to retain was determined using the Monte Carlo parallel analysis procedure (Matsunaga 2010). The resulting minimum eigenvalue for inclusion of the factor varied between 1.2 and 1.5.

With regards to the strength of factor loadings, we consider it sufficiently strong at a .4, with secondary criteria for cross-loadings above .2. We decided on a relatively low threshold value (as explained by Matsunaga 2010) to separate the clear low loadings from the midrange and high ones. Previous research on the PAQ has shown some variation in choice of threshold, and .4 is consistent with other work on the PAQ and BSRI (Choi 2004; Helmreich, Spence, and Wilhelm 1981). We report all loadings in table 2.3 to allow the reader to interpret the reliability of our measures.

First, we describe the masculinity and femininity subscales, examining each factor from left to right in turn, as presented in table 2.3. For the analysis of all respondents, depicted in the two leftmost columns of table 2.3, the F scale items loaded strongly on a single feminine factor (at least a .4 on the intended factor), except for "emotional." We also observed very small cross-loadings with the masculinity factor for the F scale items. The strongest cross-loading was -.18 for "gentle," meaning that the items intended to be of the femininity scale were clearly better fits to it than to masculinity. In the next column, the masculinity factor had overall lower factor loadings in the full sample with the M scale items, with two marginal loadings between .3 and .4 for "independent" and "feels superior." As with the F scale, there were no strong cross-loadings onto the femininity factor.

In table 2.3, we present an isolated analysis of the men in our sample. The results for the F scale closely mirror the analysis of all respondents. "Emotional" remained weakly associated with the other traits, with the rest of the scale fitting well with the intended factor and not onto the masculinity factor. The masculinity factor, among males, had an increased loading for "independent" (.47), leaving "feels superior" as the only trait indicating a poor fit. "Never gives up easily," at .41, is also lower than the full sample.

Table 2.3 also presented an isolated analysis for the women in our sample. Among women, the loading for "emotional" was the lowest among all three analyses, with a .19 loading for the femininity scale and a -.27 loading for the masculinity factor. The remaining traits on the femininity scale fit well into the feminine factor for women. For the masculinity scale, the factor loadings for "independent," "active," and "feels superior" loaded weakly, below .4, among women. Of these, "active" failed to load above .4 only for women. Alternately, the "active" trait had a strong .54 loading for men, indicating a different meaning of "active" compared to other masculine traits for women relative to men.

Overall, the PAQ showed a clear two-factor solution, separating the masculine and feminine traits. A couple of traits showed weak factor loadings, with no major cross-loadings between factors. The same factor structure held for both men and women. Men and women are similar in their levels of masculinity, but women identify stronger with femininity than men. Through our review of other analyses of the PAQ, as well as our own independent analysis, we are confident that the PAQ is an appropriate measure of a masculine gender personality, and that it is a valid and reliable instrument.

Survey Design

The survey instrument contains 76 questions covering a variety of topics, split roughly into the following categories: gender personality; candidate emergence measures; contextual political factors (table 2.4); and demographics (table 2.5). The full survey is included in the appendix. Not all questions are used in our analyses. Our survey includes the PAQ battery, discussed above, to measure masculine and feminine personality. We capture candidate emergence outcomes by asking about respondents' progressive political ambition (progressive ambition, since those in our sample are sitting city councilmembers), their perceptions of their political skills and qualifications for Congress, and experience with recruitment contact. We discuss measurement of these variables in chapter 3 (qualifications and skills), chapter 4 (recruitment), and chapter 5 (progressive ambition). We also ask respondents about their current political office and the perception of the competitiveness of their local and congressional districts, which we refer to as "contextual political factors." Last, we measure demographic variation between respondents, such as their sex, age, income, religion, education, race, and party identification.

Contextual variables are summarized in table 2.4, including electoral competitiveness and partisanship. We account for perceived competitiveness of local and congressional elections with two measures. Previous research has shown that the opportunity structure, including how competitive elections are, influences not only progressive ambition but also the efforts of recruiters to seek out candidates (Maestas et al. 2006; Moncrief, Squire, and Jewell 2001; Sanbonmatsu 2006). Respondents rated the competitiveness of local and congressional elections from not at all competitive to very competitive.

Party identification is an important control variable, used in all models. It is clear that more women run as Democrats than as Republicans (CAWP 2017), and there are important partisan dimensions to political office, especially at the state and national level. People who identify with minor parties are unlikely to run or be as successful in a strong two-party system, so while local office has room for nonpartisans, higher office is much more restrictive. To control for the effects of party, we code party identification with two dummy variables, one for identifying as a Democrat and one for identifying as a Republican, with Independent identification as the baseline. The variables shown in regression tables should be interpreted as the difference between Democrats and Independents, and Republicans and Independents. This comparison would be obscured with a single ordinal variable because Independents may change the linear relationship in this context. By comparing Democrats and Republicans to Independents, who are expected to be at a disadvantaged position in the political opportunity structure given the two-party system, it allows us to observe the effects of an association with a major political party in a clearer way than would a single variable for partisanship.

TABLE 2.4. Descriptive Statistics for Contextual Variables

Category	N	Percent
Competitiveness: Local Elections		
Very Competitive	148	21.4
Competitive	246	35.5
Somewhat Competitive	267	38.5
Not at All Competitive	32	4.6
Competitiveness: Congressional Elections		
Very Competitive	266	38.3
Competitive	188	27.1
Somewhat Competitive	155	22.3
Not at All Competitive	85	12.2
Party Identification		
Strong Democrat	174	25.6
Leaning Democrat	129	19.0
Independent/No Party	111	16.3
Leaning Republican	135	19.9
Strong Republican	130	19.1

We control for demographic characteristics in our analytical models throughout the book. We present a summary of demographics in our sample in table 2.5. The majority of our sample is married (80 percent). Therefore, we control for marital status using a dummy variable, where we split married individuals from individuals identifying as single, widowed, separated, divorced, and unmarried but living as a couple. We control for marital status because research has shown that being married has a positive effect on political ambition, particularly for men and those with supportive spouses (Crowder-Meyer 2018). The majority of our sample has an associate's degree or higher (80 percent). We account for respondent education because education is an objective indicator of candidate quality. We also control for respondent age. About 80 percent of our sample is 50 or older; 20.2 percent of the sample is over 70 years old. Previous scholarship finds age to be an important factor in predicting women's decision to run—women are more likely to run later in life (Thomas 2002; Fulton et al. 2006).

Given our relatively older sample, there is a somewhat nonlinear relationship between age and the outcomes of interest. For example, a young city councilmember may enter the city council after completing college at the beginning of their potentially long political career, much like the image of the political career ladder described by Schlesinger (1966). On the other hand, a person may enter the city council after retirement, as an expression of their familiarity with their city. This councilmember would be unlikely to run for any other office in the future. People between these extremes vary in their average likelihood of entering office. The result of this pattern is an overall negative sign to the linear relationship between age and outcomes related to running for higher office. As a control variable,[2] rather than an independent variable of interest, we will not make clear inferences about these relationships, but it is an area of potential future study.

We asked respondents to identify their race: 88.2 percent of our sample identified as white; 6 percent identified as Black; and 2.7 percent as Latino; less than 1 percent identified as Asian (0.9) and Native American (0.8), while only 1.4 percent as a race we did not list (see table 2.5). Therefore, we collapse our race measurement into two dummy variables that target racial differences for Black and Latino respondents, with all others as the

---

2. We replicated a number of analyses with the log of age in place of age as the control variable, with no change in the results of the main independent variables of interest. We also ran analyses excluding the group of respondents over the age of 70 who on average had the lowest levels of progressive ambition. This also did not change the outcomes of interest. Therefore, we retained the variable as the respondent's age, including respondents across the age spectrum.

baseline category. In the analyses, the variables for Black and Latino can be interpreted as comparing that target group to the rest of the sample. There are some limitations to this as our mechanism for analyzing racial and ethnic differences. Given the size of our sample, there are not enough responses to have quality interaction variables or to run subgroup analysis of nonwhite respondents. This limits our capacity for intersectional analysis. We will address this limitation more fully in the conclusion to the book. Our work should therefore be interpreted with this note of caution. Indeed, masculinity may operate differently for white people compared to people of color. Further research is needed to examine the ways that masculinity may operate differently for men and women of color (see Liv-

TABLE 2.5. Descriptive Statistics for Demographic Variables

Category	N	Percent
Marital Status		
Single	46	6.8
Married	543	80.3
Separated	8	1.2
Divorced	31	4.6
Unmarried, Living as a Couple	19	2.8
Widowed	25	3.7
Race/Ethnicity		
White	584	88.2
Black	40	6.0
Native American	5	0.8
Asian	6	0.9
Latino	18	2.7
Other	9	1.4
Education		
Less Than High School	2	0.3
High School	21	3.1
Some College	111	16.3
Associates or Bachelor's Degree	234	34.4
Law Degree	46	6.8
Other Graduate Degree	265	38.9
Age		
Under 40	46	6.9
40 to 49	84	12.7
50 to 59	180	27.2
60 to 69	218	32.9
70 or over	134	20.2
Sex		
Female	206	30.3
Male	473	69.7

ingston, Rosette, and Washington 2012; Frederick 2013, 2014; Shah, Scott, and Juenke 2019).

Empirical Analyses

In chapters 3, 4, and 5 we present original analysis examining the relationship between gender personality and city councilmembers' self-perceived qualification to run for Congress, their experiences with recruitment, and whether they will run for higher office. In chapter 3, we address self-perceived qualifications and political skills. We develop our theory that masculine councilmembers, both men and women, who report high levels of masculinity will feel more qualified to run for Congress than those with relatively low masculinity. The masculine traits override gender role expectations for women and help to close the gap in qualifications between men and women. Therefore, we expect a positive relationship between masculine personality and perceptions of qualification for all sexes.

In chapter 4, we present an analysis of the relationship between gender personality and recruitment experience. We expected to find a positive relationship between masculinity and recruitment; people who are more masculine should be rewarded, in that they are more likely to be recruited regardless of their sex. In chapter 5, we link masculinity to progressive political ambition, through an indirect model. Building on findings in the previous chapters, those who are more masculine feel more qualified and are recruited at higher rates, and then those features drive their increased progressive ambition. Moreover, the bridge between masculinity and ambition through the mediators of self-perceived qualification and recruitment also helps to explain differences between men and women in their ambitions for higher office. Masculine personality is the antecedent for perceptions of qualification, shapes individuals' interactions with other political actors in the recruitment process, and explains why some people start at the city council level to launch their upward political career, and others do not.

Conclusion

Our review of the previous literature on self-perceived qualifications for political office, and political recruitment experiences, points to an inherent association with gender. Whether it be through the specific appeals made by recruiters or notions of what it takes to run for political office, masculine norms pervade these processes. And although previous scholarship has acknowledged the political terrain as gendered, much of the observational analysis has relied on differences between men and women to draw it out.

Our data comes from a sample of city councilmembers from around the United States who were asked a series of questions that allow us to delineate more masculine from more feminine individuals and to draw a direct connection between gender personality and successful candidate emergence. Therefore, we can more precisely identify gender—in particular, masculinity—as a source of women's underrepresentation in American politics. Moreover, our analysis will contribute to a greater understanding of the gender hierarchy in American politics and whether institutions place a premium on masculine qualities, behaviors, and approaches to problems, at the expense of femininity and to the detriment of stereotypically feminine women.

Our approach to studying candidate emergence by incorporating gender personality adds an additional layer for understanding the candidate emergence process and women's experiences. Although our conceptualization of gender personality is personal and psychological, we argue that we can account for internal and external routes to progressive ambition with this variable. The internal route toward political ambition is the relationship between self-perceived qualifications and ambition. The external route toward ambition is between recruitment contact and ambition. Our theory is that masculinity is the nexus of internal and external routes of political ambition. By analyzing gender personality, we explore a personality-driven explanation for predicting an individual's experience during the candidate emergence process that accounts for both of these routes.

What are the consequences of our findings? Beyond contributing to the explanations for the underrepresentation of women as a group in American politics, our study speaks to the lack of gender diversity of elected officials, among both men and women. Independent of the effect of sex directly, masculinity affects an individuals' experience during the candidate emergence process, such as the decision to run for office, which limits the range of gender expressions, qualities, and values in office, particularly at high levels. If the masculine barriers to elected office do not change then there will be a continued gap in women willing to run for office due to the barrier of masculinity, and potential ceiling effects as women enter the domain, if they do not differ substantially from men. This lack of gender diversity also has likely consequences on legislative approaches to public policy problems, and the breadth of solutions considered by elected representatives, which has far-reaching effects on the public at large. We address these consequences more fully in the concluding chapter of the book.

THREE

Am I Qualified?

Masculine Personality and Perceptions of Qualification

Among the surge of women running for Congress in the 2018 midterm elections were a number of Iraq and Afghanistan war veterans, like Marine Corps veteran Amy McGrath (D, KY-6) and Air Force veteran Gina Ortiz Jones (D, TX-23). Many of these women ran in open primaries against other qualified candidates, but handily won their party's nomination. For example, Navy veteran Mikie Sherrill (D, NJ-11) advanced to the general election with 70 percent of the vote; Jones claimed 68 percent in her primary runoff; and Elaine Luria (D, VA-2), a Navy veteran, won 62 percent of primary voters.

A feature of each of these women's campaigns was their military experience. Amy McGrath's viral campaign video, "Told Me," is focused on her experience as a Marine. In a voice-over, while images of explosions are on screen, McGrath says, "I spent 20 years as a US marine, flew 89 combat missions bombing Al Qaeda and the Taliban. I was the first woman marine to fly in an F-18 in combat, and I got to land on aircraft carriers." Mikie Sherrill also describes her military experience in her ad "Grandfather": "I went to the Naval Academy, graduated into flight school in the first class of women eligible for combat, and became a Sea King helicopter pilot, flying missions in Europe and the Middle East." And Elaine Luria describes how her experiences as a Naval officer qualify her for Congress: "I spent 20 years in the Navy, and that experience taught me that you don't live with chaos, you end it." Indeed, former military personnel regularly run and win elections by emphasizing the ways that their military service qualifies them for public service as elected officials. Veterans make up a smaller share of elected members today than in the past. According to an analysis by Pew Research Center, "Between 1965 and 1975, at least 70% of lawmakers in each legislative chamber had military experience" (Gieger, Bialik, and Gramlich 2019). Today, that number is about 18 percent. Still, former military make up about 7 percent of the U.S. adult population; therefore, veterans are overrepresented in Congress. But it is only in the last decade or so that women have been able to serve in the military to a similar degree as men, and to leverage that experience and those qualifications in their bid for political office.

Women veterans who run for office are uniquely positioned to tout their experiences in a masculine field, like the military, and the character traits that they developed in their military roles, like toughness, strength, stamina, and leadership. Not only are these characteristics and traits that voters revere, they may explain why women veterans see themselves as qualified to run for office in the first place. As previous studies have shown, the self-perception that individuals are qualified to run for office is eminently important in their decision to run. As Lawless and Fox (2010, 116) note, self-perceived qualification is "the most potent explanation we uncovered for the gender gap in political ambition." Their study finds men are more likely than women to see themselves as qualified to run for office, which contributes to the lower levels of political ambition among women. Building on this and other scholarship, we argue that self-perceived qualification differences are not simply explained by individuals' sex but also by their gender personality. Although previous studies have attempted to uncover the origins of the self-perceived qualification gap between men and women, a focus on sex differences means that this scholarship has inadvertently missed an opportunity to assess the role of masculine and feminine personality traits for explaining this gap. We anticipate that women (and men) who are more masculine will be more likely to see themselves as qualified to run for office, given the theoretical congruency between their personal strengths (more masculine) and the perception of political careers (requiring masculinity). Women veterans jumping into the fray to run for political office is just one possible illustration of this congruence effect, especially insofar as women with military experience possess more masculine personalities than women without military experience.

In this chapter, we describe the prevalence of the qualifications gap, which is the gap in men's and women's perceptions that they are qualified to run for public office. Previous studies find that similarly situated men and women differ in their views about whether they are qualified; men are twice as likely as women to view themselves as qualified (Lawless and Fox 2010; see also Pruysers and Blais 2019). We argue that one understudied factor for explaining the qualification gap is gender personality, and that gender personality contributes to variation in perceptions of qualification, which manifest as differences between men's and women's interest in running for political office. We expect that an individual with a more masculine personality, regardless of sex, will be more likely to perceive themselves as qualified for political office. We expect a positive relationship between masculine personality and perceptions of qualification for political office, because of the perception that political positions privilege masculine traits, such as confidence, assertiveness, and requiring masculine behaviors like self-promotion and dealing with conflict (Schneider et al. 2016). Therefore, we expect congruence between masculine personalities and masculine positions.

Gender personality holds vast appeal for explaining individuals' perception that they are qualified to run for political office. It makes intuitive sense that masculine individuals would be more likely to see themselves as better suited for roles that have come to be defined as masculine and as fulfilling masculine goals, like public office, than would feminine, or less masculine, individuals. We rely on our survey of city councilmembers to assess whether a masculine personality will predict positive perceptions of qualification for Congress, for men and women. Therefore, as discussed in chapter 2, our sample represents individuals who have already emerged as candidates at the local level, and we assess their perception that they are qualified to run for a higher office. Our theory is that this relationship between gender personality and perceptions of qualification explains why fewer women run for higher office and why more masculine individuals run for higher office.

Perception of Qualification and Women's Underrepresentation

Numerous explanations for women's underrepresentation exist, and foremost among them is a scant supply of women candidates (e.g., Norris 1997). If women do not run, they cannot win; so why are women less likely to run? Despite gains in women's interest in running for office over time, men still outnumber them a great deal. In 2018, when women's interest in running for political office surged, women still trailed behind men, as we showed in chapter 2 (fig. 2.1). In 2018, women only made up about 24 percent of the share of candidates running for House seats in the midterms (CAWP 2018). Although women made up less than a quarter of the candidates running for House seats in 2018, this represents a 6-percentage point increase from the previous high in 2016.

One well-established explanation for why women trail behind men in running for office is that women see themselves as less qualified for politics and government than men. This internalized bias is distinct from external sources of bias, such as the double bind, which certainly exist, and which influence women's electoral success (e.g., Teele, Kalla, and Rosenbluth 2018). As Fox and Lawless (2011, 61) show, "Highly accomplished women from both major political parties are substantially less likely than similarly situated men to perceive themselves as qualified to seek elective office." Therefore, self-perceived qualification, an individual's belief that he or she is qualified to run for political office, influences the supply of individuals willing to run for office. It makes intuitive sense that if an individual does not see themselves as qualified for a role, then they will not attempt to fill that role. Similar to the calculus a person might make when deciding to apply for a job, an individual will consider their own experiences and skills to determine if they are suited to a position (as well as whether the position meets their goals, which we will discuss in more depth in chapter 5).

Indeed, when it comes to political office, women are less likely to see their skills and experiences as qualifying. Looking at perceptions of skills that are relevant to public office, Lawless and Fox (2010) found that men were more likely than women to indicate that they are knowledgeable about public policy, have relevant professional experience, are good at public speaking and fundraising, and are good at self-promoting. But even among those "who knowingly possessed the educational, professional, and community experience to run for office," the women "concluded that they were not qualified to enter electoral politics because they had the 'wrong temperament,' 'not enough gumption' or an 'aversion to criticism'" (129). Women also said they did not think they had "thick enough skin" to run for political office, suggesting that women perceive the political environment as unfriendly and combative (Fox and Lawless 2010, 131; see Fulton 2012 for perception that the political environment is unequal). These responses are concrete evidence that many women see running for political office as necessitating masculinity. Therefore, in explaining the qualification gap, these observations provide a link to masculinity by drawing attention to the skills and traits that are perceived as necessary—which are masculine, or more likely to be developed in masculine careers—and the perception disproportionately by women that they do not possess these skills and traits.

Perhaps as a means of overcoming what they see as fewer qualifications, women are more likely to emphasize specific professional experiences when explaining whether or not they are qualified, whereas men are less likely to mention professional experience. Therefore, "women rely on a more exhaustive set of criteria when assessing whether they are qualified to run for office" (Lawless and Fox 2010, 126). This may have to do with confidence, although not necessarily in themselves; instead, women may have less confidence that the system will recognize their abilities and skills, and thus they present more evidence upfront of their qualifications, possibly anticipating that their capability will be in doubt. As Cheryl Simrell King (1995, 88) recognizes, "Unfortunately, for women, proving one's masculinity is not as easy as it is for men. Because of the deep cultural foundations of sex or gender roles, men prove their masculinity almost by default." Women's efforts to list more professional experiences may be done to shore up any suspicion that they are not qualified.

Sarah Fulton (2012) argues that making the distinction about initial qualifications is important for drawing conclusions about women and voters' perceptions of their viability in politics and government. As Fulton points out, when women perform as well as men in elections it is assumed that voters are not prejudiced against women. However, "if men and women are distinct regarding characteristics that influence their electability—for instance, if women hold higher political quality than men but only perform at parity with men in the electoral arena—then this would be evidence of gender discrimination to the extent that women have to work harder than men to achieve similar electoral results" (Fulton 2012, 304). In short, Fulton argues that previous studies suffer from selection bias, in that the women in the analysis have already overcome the steeper qualification expectations that women rely upon when evaluating their own fitness. Fulton concludes that sex parity in election outcomes is a function of qualification, because the women who do run are more qualified. Once candidates' qualifications are taken into account, men are at about a 3-point advantage. Therefore, the explanations that women are as likely to win political office as men should acknowledge this selection bias (see also Anzia and Berry 2011; O'Brien and Rickne 2016).

The effect of the qualifications gap was evident in the 2018 midterms. In their analysis of candidates running in open Democratic primaries for Congress and governor through August 2018, Conroy, Rakich, and Nguyen (2018) found that women who ran were far more likely to have previous experience as elected officials than the men running, especially if they were running for higher-profile roles, like governor or senator. Fifty-six percent of the women who ran for governorships had previous experience as elected officials, compared with just 37 percent of men who ran for governor. In Senate races, the difference was even larger—80 percent of women who ran for Senate had previously held elected office, compared with just 22 percent of men. Since previous experience as an elected official helps women to overcome the belief that they lack qualifications, it makes sense that the women running for a high-level office are more likely to have been elected before compared with men, who do not doubt their qualifications to the same degree. Whereas women question their qualifications, and likely wade into politics more deliberately, men overestimate their skills, and are less inhibited about running for political office (Fox and Lawless 2010; Carroll and Sanbonmatsu 2013). Therefore, it is widely acknowledged that men and women differ in the perception that they are qualified, and that these differences lead to variation in men's and women's enthusiasm for running for office. But why does this difference emerge?

Explaining the Qualification Gap

Previous studies have pointed to socialization differences that contribute to women's expressed lower levels of qualification. For example, Thomas (2005) suggests that differences in gender socialization as youth lead to the development of skills that are gendered and contribute to the qualification gap between men and women later in life. Socialization studies argue that attitudes and behaviors are transmitted to individuals from their environment, like the media they consume, or their peers and community. In particular, parents are an especially strong transmitter of political attitudes and behaviors (e.g., Jennings and Niemi 2014). The socialization of gender roles in particular is important to understanding variation in men's and women's political ambition. From childhood onward, individuals are taught that there are expectations linked to their sex, known as gender roles. For instance, in general, women are expected to focus on caretaking, especially of young children, while men are expected to support a family financially by working full time (Parker and Wang 2013).

Gender socialization at the societal level contributes to sex differences in gender personality. Because men and women are expected to behave differently and take on different roles in society, they internalize these expectations and manifest them as differences in gender personality. The psychological perspective on gender (e.g., Spence and Helmreich 1978; Bem 1993) defines gender personality in terms of internalization of sex-typed personality traits. Sex-typed personality traits or attributes are those that are considered more appropriate for one sex. Masculine personalities identify with instrumental traits such as aggressiveness, self-confidence, independence, and toughness, among others. Feminine personalities identify with expressive traits, such as emotionality, warmth and helpfulness toward others, compassion, and gentleness. Men tend to identify with masculine personality traits, while women tend to identify with more feminine personality traits (Bem 1993; Butterfield and Powell 2005). But as reviewed in chapter 2, individual differences in trait adoption and expression occur *among* women and men. Shifting social norms and individual-level experiences will lead to variation in the degree to which social roles are seen as male- or female-typical. Thus, although women are more likely to identify with feminine traits, and men are more likely to identify with masculine traits, men and women can and do vary in their possession of both (Twenge 1997, 2001; Spence and Buckner 2000; Donnelly and Twenge 2012). Therefore, various political behaviors correspond with masculine and feminine traits and goals *among* men and women (e.g., McDermott 2016; Schneider et al. 2016), and are not specific to one sex or the other.

One way that familial socialization imparts femininity and masculinity expectations is through parental interactions and encouragement of behaviors. Fox and Lawless (2014) observe the effects of familial gender socialization on political interest in their study of young men and women (aged 13–17 and 18–25). For example, they ask their respondents about their interactions with their parents, such as the extent to which parents discuss politics with them, under the assumption that political discussion with parents leads to greater interest in politics. Fox and Lawless report that compared to young men, young women indicate fewer political discussions with their parents; 24 percent of young men compared to 19 percent of young women indicate that their parents discuss politics with them (see also Mayer and Schmidt 2004). Young men also say they were more likely to be encouraged to seek political office than young women, by their mothers and fathers; 40 percent of male respondents, but only 29 percent of female respondents, reported encouragement to run for office later in life from at least one parent. Overall, this report finds that young men are socialized to be more politically active and interested in politics than young women.

In addition to differences in political discussion between young men and women, young men receive more encouragement than young women do to participate in competitive experiences, highlighting another means by which youth gender socialization leads to the development of skills that are gendered and contribute to the qualification gap between men and women later in life. Competitive experiences, like athletic contests, encourage winning and familiarize participants with conflict and confrontation, which are masculine behaviors. The competitive experiences afforded by athletic contests are akin to the competitive experiences in the political environment, especially an election. Therefore, it comes as no surprise that young women and men who are exposed to competitive experiences, such as participation in athletics, show a heightened interest in running for public office (Fox and Lawless 2014). Yet due to the greater encouragement young men receive to participate in these endeavors, the benefits of competitive experiences are lopsided. Regardless, the fact that young women who participate in competitive extracurricular activities also show greater interest in politics supports our thesis that masculine behaviors elicit interest in the masculine domain of political careers, irrespective of individuals' sex.

Congruence between masculine personality traits and masculine career fields has been observed by scholars interested in the underrepresentation of women in science, technology, engineering, and math (STEM). Studies find that the belief that STEM fields are masculine leads young women to lose interest because they assume they lack the qualifications for STEM careers (e.g., Diekman and Steinberg 2013). Although women have experienced rapid advances in many professional roles in recent decades, women remain underrepresented in STEM professions (Diekman, Weisgram, and Belanger 2015), and the origins of this underrepresentation are similar to the source of women's underrepresentation in politics. Scholars who study STEM begin with childhood socialization of gender roles. For instance, although girls and boys engage in STEM-related activities at a similar rate, they vary in terms of their activities and the encouragement they receive from adults. For example, encouraged by gender stereotypes, boys are more likely to engage with tools (e.g., microscopes) and girls with planting (e.g., growing food) (Jones et al. 2010), and parents provide boys with more opportunities to learn about STEM than girls. Moreover, these opportunities are contingent upon expressed interest for girls but not for boys (Alexander, Johnson, and Kelley 2012; Crowley et al. 2001).

These gender socialized views of STEM lead women to hold negative attitudes toward the field (Nosek, Banaji, and Greenwald 2002; Lane, Goh, and Driver-Linn 2012; Correll 2001). A recent study from the American Association of University Women finds that girls and women who internalize the stereotype of STEM pursuits as suited for men see themselves as less competent than men in math (AAUW 2015). From the STEM literature we observe that norms contribute to the notion that STEM is a masculine domain, and gender socialization leads to adherence to traditional notions of gender roles for men and women within these fields. Therefore,

STEM fields are seen as incongruent with gender roles associated with women, and thus women are less likely to view themselves as qualified for these careers in these fields. However, it is our argument that the incongruence would be more prominent for feminine individuals than it would be for women in general.

The same sort of internalized gender attributes and role congruence effects that we observe in STEM can be extrapolated to form expectations about internalized gender attributes and political careers. Given the perception of politics as a largely masculine domain (e.g., Schneider et al. 2016), we should expect masculine individuals to view themselves as more qualified for a political career than less masculine individuals. In the next section, we assess the relationship between masculine personality and perceptions of qualifications for political office.

Analysis: Perception of Qualification and Gender Personality

Does gender personality correlate with city councilmembers' perceptions that they are qualified to run for Congress? As we outline in chapter 2, city councilmembers' gender personality is measured with the Personality Attributes Questionnaire, which probes an individual's self-identification with associated qualities such as "confidence" and "aggression" for masculinity, and "devotion to others" and "warmth" for femininity (Spence and Helmreich 1978).

Scant attention has been paid to how potential candidates' own internalized identification as masculine or feminine affects the supply of candidates for political office. Perception of qualification is a classic supply-side variable, where individuals' internalized notions of their skills and qualification should influence whether or not they are interested in running for public office. We expect that variation among men and women found by measuring gender personality will offer an underlying explanation for individual-level differences in perceived qualification and political skills. We anticipate that women and men who are more masculine will view themselves as more qualified for public office than women and men who are less masculine.

Measurement

To measure the concept of qualifications for political office, our survey asks respondents, who are sitting city councilmembers, to indicate their self-perceived qualifications to run for Congress, a more prestigious office. Respondents were asked to indicate the degree to which they thought of themselves as qualified to run for Congress on a four-point scale ranging from "very unqualified" to "very qualified." The question does not directly measure objective considerations of qualifications, such as political skills or experience, but rather taps into individuals' subjective perception of their own qualifications. This allows us to assess the hypothesis that masculinity is positively associated with an internal sense of ability. The qualification measure is similar to the measure used by Fox and Lawless (2011) in their study of working professionals' political ambition.

We specifically identify Congress because individuals in our respondent pool currently serve on the city council. Our goal in constructing our question was to make the measure similar to previous studies on this topic so that comparison is possible. For example, Fox and Lawless (2011) asked more generally if respondents felt qualified to hold any elected office, but they surveyed individuals who did not have political experience. Therefore, our self-perceived qualification question deals with qualifications for a position our respondents do not hold, and for a position that would likely require more objective skills than the position they currently occupy. Our measure sets a higher bar by specifying Congress, compared to previous research on self-perceived qualification. We take this approach because it also standardizes respondents' focus on one office (Congress), which is useful, given that different offices have different barriers for qualifications (Carroll and Sanbonmatsu 2013; Fowler 1996). For instance, the qualities affiliated with the presidency are different from the qualities affiliated with Congress or a state legislative seat (e.g., Streb et al. 2008).

Findings

Descriptive analysis of our measure of self-perceived qualifications indicate that most respondents in our pool of city councilmembers consider themselves either "qualified" or "somewhat qualified" to run for Congress. The average response to whether an individual in our sample thought they were qualified to run for Congress is 2.6 out of 4 ($SD = .95$; $Mdn = 3$). Only 13.8 percent view themselves as unqualified to run for Congress. Descriptive statistics for this variable are presented in figure 3.1.

Consistent with previous scholarship, we find men report significantly higher levels of perceived qualifications; men average 2.7 out of 4 ($SD = .94$), while women average 2.4 ($SD = .95$, $\chi^2 = 19.3$, $p < .001$). As displayed in figure 3.2, women are more likely to report the two lowest categories

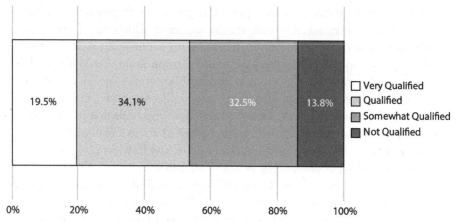

Fig. 3.1. Perception of Qualifications for Congress
(*Note:* Responses to "How qualified or unqualified do you feel you are to run for Congress?")

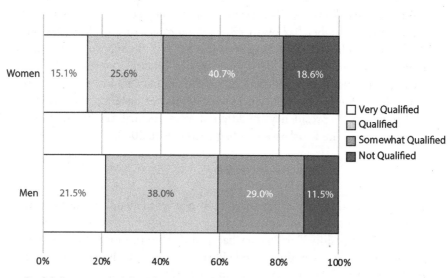

Fig. 3.2. Perception of Qualifications for Congress for Men and Women
(*Note:* Men's and Women's responses to "How qualified or unqualified do you feel you are to run for Congress?")

on the scale (59.3 percent), while men are more likely to report the two higher categories of qualifications (59.5 percent). This difference in perceived qualifications between men and women replicates prior research on the qualifications gap and sex differences (e.g., Lawless and Fox 2010; Fox and Lawless 2011). However, differences in perceived qualifications between men and women do not tell the whole story; as our analysis will show, masculine gender personality helps to explain a sizeable portion of the bivariate effect of sex.

Masculine Personality and Perception of Qualifications

Descriptive analysis indicates that there are marked differences in perceptions of qualification for our measure of masculine personality. In figure 3.3 we present average qualification perceptions for those who scored above the median masculinity score (24) compared to those who scored below the median masculinity score. On average, individuals who score at or below the median masculinity score for the group indicate their qualifications for Congress as 2.38, compared to 2.86 for those who score above the median masculinity score for our sample; this difference is statistically significant ($p = .001$).

Differences in perception of qualifications for those with high and low feminine personality are insignificant (figure 3.4). On average, individuals who score below the median femininity score (24) indicate their qualifications for Congress as 2.58, compared to 2.65 for those who score above the median femininity score for our sample; this difference is not statistically significant ($p = .45$).

To uncover whether masculine personality influences perceptions of qualification to run for Congress we specify an OLS regression model. We find that those with more masculine personalities perceive themselves as more qualified to run for Congress than individuals with less masculine personalities, even when accounting for sex. Table 3.1 presents the relationship between gender personality and perceptions of qualification. There are four separate models in table 3.1, which test different specifications. Model 1 presents the fully specified model. Model 2 excludes the gender personality measures; Models 3 and 4 subset to women and men, respectively. In Model 1, we present our full model, with sex and gender personality, as well as a set of control variables, as predictors of perceived qualifications for Congress (for more on the selection of control variables, see chapter 2). As our results show, masculinity exerts a positive and significant effect ($b = .05, p < .001$). Changing from least to most masculine on a single item leads to almost a quarter point higher on the four-point qualifications scale, with

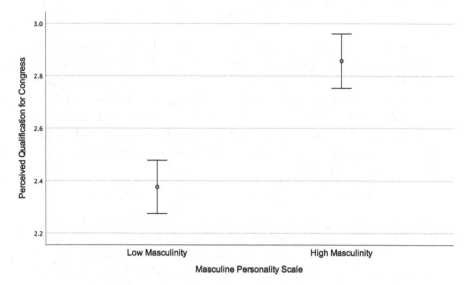

Fig. 3.3. Masculine Personality and Perceptions of Qualifications
(*Note:* Difference in mean "perceived qualification" (scale 1–4) is significant across categories of low and high masculinity (scale from 1–32). "Low Masculinity" consists of individuals who score at or below the median (24) on our measure of masculinity (N = 313); "High Masculinity" consists of individuals who score above the median on our measure of masculinity (N = 312).)

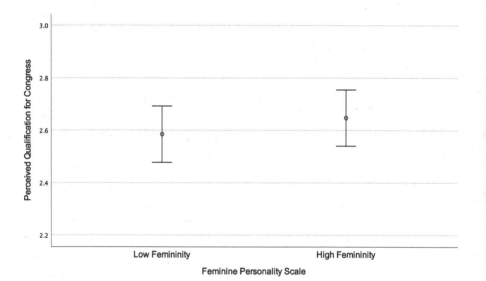

Fig. 3.4. Feminine Personality and Perceptions of Qualifications
(*Note:* Difference in mean "perceived qualification" (scale 1–4) is insignificant across categories of low and high femininity (scale from 1–32). "Low Femininity" consists of individuals who score below the median (24) on our measure of femininity (N = 373); "High Femininity" consists of individuals who score at or above the median on our measure of femininity (N = 248).)

a maximum effect of 1.4 points on the 4-point qualifications scale. The effect is significant across all model specifications in table 3.1 in which this variable is included. This finding is consistent with and expands on initial evidence from Fox and Lawless (2011) that those with "thick enough skin" are more likely to see themselves as qualified for politics and government. In their analysis, a single trait indicator of a masculine quality also had a significant effect, but the effect of our more complete scale of masculine gender personality exerts a stronger effect on the outcome and presents a more complete test of the link between gender personality and perceived qualification.

Masculine personality is not the only variable that predicts self-perceived qualifications in our full model (Model 1). As displayed in table 3.1, sex is a significant predictor; women are less likely to feel qualified than men ($b = .37, p < .001$), consistent with Lawless and Fox (2010) and Fox and

TABLE 3.1. Ordinary Least Squares Regression Predicting Self-Reported Qualifications

Variable	Model 1: Full Model		Model 2: Excludes Gender		Model 3: Only Women		Model 4: Only Men	
Gender								
Masculinity	.05	(.01)***			.03	(.02)*	.06	(.01)***
Femininity	-.01	(.01)			-.03	(.02)	.00	(.01)
Sex (Male)	.37	(.08)***	.43	(.08)***				
Political Context								
Democrat	.03	(.11)	.03	(.11)	.05	(.20)	.01	(.13)
Republican	-.01	(.11)	-.03	(.10)	-.18	(.21)	.03	(.13)
Recruitment	.12	(.02)***	.13	(.02)***	.13	(.03)***	.11	(.02)***
Local Competitiveness	.17	(.04)***	.16	(.04)***	.21	(.07)*	.15	(.06)**
Congressional Competitiveness	-.02	(.04)	-.01	(.03)	-.07	(.05)	.02	(.04)
Individual Characteristics								
Income (2011)	.07	(.03)*	.09	(.03)**	.07	(.05)	.06	(.04)
Age	.01	(.00)	.01	(.00)	.01	(.01)	.00	(.00)
Black	-.07	(.16)	.04	(.16)	.07	(.27)	-.19	(.20)
Latino	-.21	(.22)	-.12	(.22)	.05	(.30)	-.45	(.31)
Married	-.11	(.10)	-.18	(.10)	-.35	(.14)*	.08	(.13)
Education	.22	(.05)***	.26	(.50)***	.32	(.09)***	.16	(.06)**
(Constant)	-.44	(.40)	.33	(.30)	-.44	(.40)	.08	(.55)
R^2	.26		.23		.26		.26	
N	543		582		171		372	

Note: Unstandardized regression coefficients with standard errors in parentheses. Dependent variable in each model is the 4-point scale of qualifications from "very unqualified" to "very qualified."

$p < .05$, $p < .01$, $p < .001$

Lawless (2011). Income is also a significant positive predictor, where those who report higher income also report greater perceived qualifications (b = .07, $p < .01$). More educated respondents also report higher levels of qualifications (b = .22, $p < .001$). Recruitment, an external source of validation of qualifications, is also associated with higher self-perceived qualifications (b = .12, $p < .001$). More competitive local races also increase perceptions of qualification, indicating that more experience in a tough previous election builds confidence in the ability to run for Congress (b = .17, $p < .001$). This is consistent with the tendency for competitive congressional candidates to have prior office-holding experience (Fulton 2012).

We also estimate a model (Model 2 in table 3.1) that excludes gender personality. Compared to Model 2, Model 1 explains more of the variation in perception of qualification and reduces the apparent effect of sex. Adding masculine and feminine personality to the regression model increases the r^2 value by .03, a small but visible difference. Also, as expected, some of the sex difference in perceived qualifications is explained by gender personality. In both Models 1 and 2, men view themselves as more qualified than women, but in Model 1, by including the gender personality measures, the role of sex is smaller, but still significant.

Models 3 and 4 of table 3.1 test the effect of gender personality on perceived qualifications among men and women separately. These models test whether the effect of masculine personality, as well as the other control variables, varies between men and women. The effect of masculine personality is significant for both men and women (women: b = .03, $p < .05$; men: b = .06, $p < .001$). The effect is substantively larger for men, but the difference in p-values is likely due to there being more men in the sample than women. Feminine personality has no significant effect for either sex or in any model in which it is included. These variations in the magnitude of the effect of masculinity between men and women indicate an interaction between sex and gender in predicting qualifications. However, there are still no interactions between femininity and masculinity, or overall any effect of femininity on perceived qualifications.

Another way of looking at the effect of sex and gender personality on perceived qualifications is to look at what factors are associated with having the lowest and highest levels of perceived qualifications. To examine the predictors of low and high qualifications, we ran a logistic regression (table 3.2). In the first model, the dependent variable is split into those in the lowest category of qualifications ("Very Unqualified") and those with higher perceived qualifications. In the second model, on the right, the dependent variable is split between those with the highest level of perceived qualifications ("Very Qualified") and those with lower levels.

Assessing the factors that predict the lowest and highest perception of qualifications in table 3.2 suggests there is variation in the effects of both sex and masculinity. Masculine respondents are more likely to rate themselves as "very qualified" to run for Congress, mirroring our earlier analysis and the pattern in figure 3.3 ($b = .17, p < .001$). In predicting feeling "very unqualified" to run for Congress, however, masculinity is not a significant predictor. The direction is negative, as expected, but not significant ($b = -.06, p > .05$). Sex is significant in predicting the lowest rating of qualifications, with women more likely than men to rate themselves as "not at all qualified" ($b = -.64, p < .05$). Sex also predicts feeling highly qualified ($b = .80, p < .01$). Education and recruitment also exert significant effects on both low and high qualifications.

TABLE 3.2. Binary Logistic Regression Predicting Self-Reported Qualifications

Variable	Self-Reported Qualifications			
	("Very Unqualified" to Run for Congress)		("Very Qualified" to Run for Congress)	
Gender				
Masculinity	−.06	(.04)	.17	(.04)***
Femininity	.05	(.04)	−.00	(.03)
Sex (Male)	−.64	(.32)*	.80	(.29)**
Political Context				
Democrat	.63	(.43)	.18	(.38)
Republican	.52	(.42)	−.03	(.38)
Recruitment	−.53	(.09)***	.15	(.06)*
Local Competitiveness	−.43	(.18)*	.40	(.15)**
Congressional Competitiveness	−.15	(.15)	−.07	(.11)
Individual Characteristics				
Income (2011)	−.01	(.13)	.20	(.11)
Age	−.01	(.01)	.02	(.01)
Black	.16	(.71)	.20	(.49)
Latino	.05	(.91)	.06	(.70)
Married	.02	(.37)	−.38	(.32)
Education	−.77	(.20)***	.64	(.19)***
(Constant)	3.59	(1.59)*	−11.17	(1.59)***
Cox & Snell R^2	.15		.15	
N	543		543	

Note: Binary logistic regression coefficients with standard errors in parentheses.

*$p < .05$, **$p < .01$, ***$p < .001$

Masculine Personality and Political Skills

In addition to our measure of self-perceived qualifications for higher office, we also asked about specific skills related to running for and holding political office. We included the same set of skills as Fox and Lawless (2011) in our survey: policy knowledge, fundraising, public speaking, professional experience, self-promotion, and political connections. These are all specific skills that would help a candidate in running for high-level political office, and should predict whether a person has overall confidence in their qualifications (see Fulton 2012). Previous work has shown that even with equitable levels of skills, men tend to overestimate their capabilities and women tend to minimize theirs (Fox and Lawless 2011). We note that these skills might be gendered, although not overtly. In particular, "self-promotion" is a masculine behavior (Schneider et al. 2016). Political connections and professional experiences are more likely to be afforded to those in masculine careers or fields, but we do not directly observe the perception that these skills are viewed as masculine or feminine by our respondents.

Previous research finds men are more likely than women to perceive of themselves as possessing political skills (Fox and Lawless 2011). This gap between men and women may be due to women's tendency to underestimate their experience and undervalue their achievements, or because men tend to be overconfident (see Fox and Lawless 2011 for a review). Masculinity may underscore these differences. Indeed, those who are masculine have higher levels of overall confidence, which should translate to the type of overestimation of skills seen in research on men and women (Elder 2004). Masculine individuals likely see themselves as more qualified for the types of jobs and projects that build political skills for the same reasons that masculine individuals are drawn to competitive political careers.

Although men were more confident in their possession of most of the political skills we asked about, analysis of our pool shows that of the six political skill questions, there were statistically significant sex differences on only two. Men were more likely to report having strong policy knowledge (+ 12.2%, χ^2 = 9.02, $p < .05$) and professional experience (+ 9%, χ^2 = 4.82, $p < .01$). For all other skills—public speaking ability, fundraising, self-promotion skills, and political connections—male and female city councilmembers report similar levels of possession (table 3.3). Our results differ from Fox and Lawless (2011), which found significant gaps in perception of skills between men and women for each of these. However, Fox and Lawless asked generally well-qualified individuals these questions, whereas we survey city councilmembers who may be better able to judge their capacity to carry out these skills. Also, this population overall has a higher level of skills than average, which works to minimize sex differences.

On average, the overall number of skills respondents indicate they possess shows that there is an insignificant difference in the number reported between men and women (M_{women} = 2.74; M_{men} = 2.96; χ^2 = 4.97; p = .55). This is a departure from the results on overall assessment of qualifications (figure 3.3), where men were shown to indicate perception of qualifications to a greater degree than women. Yet, when broken down into the individual components of the qualifications arguably necessary to run for office, for our pool men and women differ only slightly. This finding leads us to suggest that individual skills translate into a global assessment of being qualified for men differently than for women.

Next, we turn to differences in reporting political skills between more and less masculine individuals. As we anticipated, we find that masculinity predicts reporting political skills, and this relationship is more robust than the relationship between political skill and candidate sex. Descriptive analysis indicates that there are marked differences in indication of possession of skills by masculine personality. In figure 3.5 we present the average number of identified skills for those who scored above the median masculinity score versus those who scored below the median masculinity score. On average, individuals who score below the median masculinity score for the group indicate that they possess 2.41 skills, compared to 3.42 for those who score above the median masculinity score for our sample; this difference is statistically significant (p = .001).

Feminine personality exerts no influence on indicating possession of skills (figure 3.6). On average, individuals who score below the median femininity score for the group indicate they possess 2.82 skills, compared

TABLE 3.3. Sex Differences in Perceived Political Skills

Political Skills	Percent Yes	
	Women	Men
Policy Knowledge	54.5%	66.7%*
Fundraising	29.0%	31.1%
Public Speaking	60.0%	59.1%
Professional Experience	56.5%	65.5%**
Self-Promotion	37.0%	32.2%
Political Connections	37.0%	41.6%
None of the Above	13.5%	11.9%

Note: Numbers indicate the percentage of respondents that report possessing the given political skill. Significance of Chi-Square assessing difference between men and women: *p < .05, **p < .01.

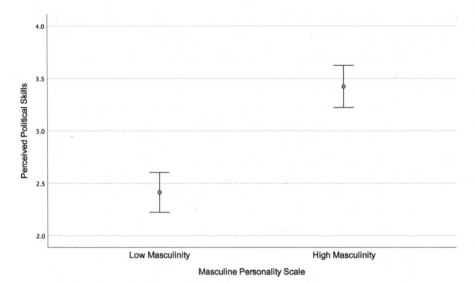

Fig. 3.5. Masculine Personality and Perceived Political Skills

(*Note:* Difference in mean "perceived political skill" (scale 0–6) is significant across categories of low and high masculinity (scale from 1–32). "Low Masculinity" consists of individuals who score at or below the median (24) on our measure of masculinity (N = 313); "High Masculinity" consists of individuals who score above the median on our measure of masculinity (N = 312).)

to 2.99 for those who score above the median femininity score. This difference is not statistically significant ($p = .25$).

We also present analysis for the correlation between masculinity, sex, perceived qualifications, and number of political skills in table 3.4. The relationship is stronger between masculinity and skills than the link between sex and skills. Sex and political skills are not significantly correlated ($r = .06$, $p = .16$); however, masculinity and political skills are positively correlated ($r = .33, p < .001$). These results suggest that individuals who possess a more masculine personality are more confident in their capacity to seek out and build competencies in the various skills that lead to high-quality candidates, or, alternatively, are more likely to exaggerate their self-perceived skills than individuals with less masculine personalities. Although we cannot necessarily eliminate the latter possibility, it should not detract from the overall conclusion, which is that masculine personality is positively correlated with an individual's belief that they possess skills deemed important for public office.

Next, we present two regression models (a limited model and a full model) for testing whether individuals indicate they possess the political

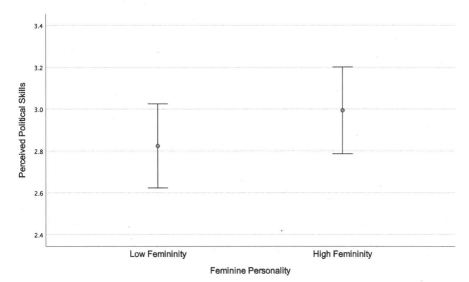

Fig. 3.6. Feminine Personality and Perceived Political Skills
(*Note:* Difference in mean "perceived political skills" (scale 0–6) is insignificant across categories of low and high femininity (scale from 1–32). "Low Femininity" consists of individuals who score below the median (24) on our measure of femininity (N = 373); "High Femininity" consists of individuals who score at or above the median on our measure of femininity (N = 248).)

TABLE 3.4. Correlations between Sex, Masculinity, Femininity, Qualifications, and Political Skills

	Male	Masculinity	Femininity	Perceived Qualifications	Political Skills
Male	1.00				
Masculinity	.05	1.00			
Femininity	−.09*	.22***	1.00		
Perceived Qualifications	.15***	.29***	.04	1.00	
Political Skills	.06	.33***	.04	.47***	1.00

Note: Bivariate Correlation Coefficients; *p < .05, **p < .01, ***p < .001

skills we include in our survey (table 3.5). In our limited model, where we only include masculinity, femininity, and sex as predictors of affirming the possession of political skills, masculinity, but not sex, exerts a significant effect. In table 3.5, our dependent variable is a continuous variable that varies from 0 to 6, where "0" indicates that respondents do not believe they possess any of the skills we list, versus "6" where respondents indicate that they possesses all six of the skills from our list. Our results show that a one-point increase in masculinity leads to a .17 increase in number of reported skills (b = .17, p < .001). Identifying as a man, on the other hand, adds .11 additional skills, which does not approach statistical significance. Therefore, a one-point increase on the scale of masculine personality has a greater effect than the difference between being a woman and being a man. After adding a set of control variables (Full Model), masculinity remains a significant positive predictor of a number of perceived skills (b = .11, p < .001). In this model, sex is also significant; (b = .42, p < .01). We interpret this finding to point to recruitment and education acting as suppressor variables, where men report more skills, but only after accounting for education and recruitment.

In our Full Model we observe additional predictors of the belief by individuals that they possess political skills; our model finds political recruitment, higher levels of education, party affiliation as a Democrat, and the competitiveness of local elections to have a positive and statistically sig-

TABLE 3.5. Ordinary Least Squares Regression Predicting Political Skills

Variable	Number of Political Skills			
	Limited Model		Full Model	
Gender				
Masculinity	.17	(.02)***	.11	(.02)***
Femininity	−.03	(.02)	−.01	(.02)
Sex (Male)	.11	(.15)	.42	(.15)**
Political Context				
Democrat			.50	(.19)*
Republican			.30	(.19)
Recruitment			.32	(.03)***
Local Competitiveness			.16	(.08)*
Congressional Competitiveness			.04	(.06)
Individual Characteristics				
Income (2011)			.10	(.06)
Age			.00	(.01)
Black			−.20	(.28)
Latino			−.43	(.39)
Married			−.33	(.18)
Education			.42	(.09)***
(Constant)	−.58	(.59)	−2.90	(.72)***
R^2	.11		.34	
N	584		543	

Note: Unstandardized regression coefficients with standard errors in parentheses. Dependent variable in each model is the 4-point scale of qualifications from "very unqualified" to "very qualified."
*p < .05, **p < .01, ***p < .001

nificant effect—experience in more competitive local political structures, and interaction and encouragement from recruitment networks, likely help build confidence in the possession of these skills, which are relevant to running for political office. Individuals were not more likely to build skills in competitive congressional districts, however, with null effects for that variable.

Conclusion

Our results find masculine personality exerts a clear effect on how city councilmembers perceive themselves in terms of their fitness for higher-level political office; city councilmembers who more strongly identify as "independent," "active," and "confident" are more likely to see themselves as qualified for higher office than individuals who do not identify with these traits. Moreover, those who identify with feminine attributes like "gentle," "helpful," and "kind" are no more or less likely to see themselves as qualified to run for higher office.

Sex exerts an effect on perceptions of qualification, but the addition of masculine and feminine personality traits to the set of explanations is a stronger predictor and reduces the substantive effect of sex, when included in a model. Our results help to explain why women may not feel as qualified in a specifically gendered way that goes beyond hints at such an effect found in previous scholarship that does not directly assess a direct role for masculinity and femininity. In sum, while previous scholarship identifies the gap in men's and women' self-perceived qualifications, our study illuminates another source of that gap, and implicates gender personality. Our analysis demonstrates that the role of masculine personality in the candidate emergence process is important throughout the stages of candidate emergence. Even for individuals currently serving in city-level elected positions, those with personalities that are less masculine are more likely to doubt their qualifications to serve in Congress, while those with more masculine personalities are less likely to doubt their qualifications to serve in Congress.

Although our results suggest that individuals with masculine personalities see themselves as better suited to run for higher office, we recognize that there is no evidence that masculine individuals actually *are* more qualified to hold elected positions, or that they better perform the responsibilities of their position. Scholarship has investigated whether men and women differ in their approaches to building relationships or working with others as legislators, mayors, or governors (e.g., Tolleson-Rinehart 1991; Kathlene 1994), or on the legislation they support (e.g., Swers 2002, 2013; Gerrity Osborn and Mendez 2007; Frederick 2009, 2011). However, there has not been as much scholarship that has investigated whether feminine or masculine approaches are more or less effective. Therefore, it is our contention that the disconnect between individuals' personalities and the perception that they are qualified for a career in politics is due to misperceptions about a career in politics and what it takes to be effective in these roles.

Further research is needed to examine how conscious the connection between perceived skills and qualifications and the political environment may be, and how the environment is subjectively interpreted by potential candidates. Expanding analysis to include gender personality and perception of the political environment as gendered would help us better understand the extent and limits of the impact of masculinity on the process of becoming a viable political candidate for high-level office. In other words, while we assume less masculine individuals do not see themselves as qualified for politics because politics is seen as a masculine domain, it is possible that even if politics were seen as feminine, less masculine individuals would still be dissuaded. However, evidence from Pate and Fox (2018) suggest that when politics is framed as a community-building endeavor (a feminine pursuit), men are less interested in running. Insofar as "men" is a proxy for masculinity, our theory is supported.

Regardless, our results suggest that even as women become more integrated into politics, so long as their integration relies upon internalized masculinity, their progress may not have an effect on the gendered norms within the institutions. If representatives remain homogenous in their emphasis on masculine skills, traits, and roles, the diversification of elected institutions will be stalled. While objective signs of candidate quality affect perceived qualifications, including the extent of recruitment, education, and political skills and experience, other less directly relevant factors also have an impact, including gender personality, which may unfairly be holding women and those with more diverse gender roles back from political roles that could help further expand the representation of women and the transformation of politics into less of a man's game and a more inclusive one that is available to less masculine and more feminine men, women, and nonbinary individuals.

Moving forward, there are interventions that can help to bridge this gap between individuals' perception of their skills and attributes, and political careers. For example, there are a number of training programs that help individuals who may be interested in political office to build skills and to network. Indeed, as Sanbonmatsu (2015) reports, there has been a growth in organizations that recruit and train women to run for office. While Emily's List stands out as one of the longer serving groups working toward encouraging and supporting women-led candidacies, other groups like Ignite, She Should Run, Run for Something, Vote, Run Lead, E-pac, and Get Her Elected are just several of the newer organizations building momentum. Training programs could further build the confidence of participants by incorporating explicit curriculum on how a variety of gendered traits and expressions are valuable in office, and how campaigns can help to frame a candidate's personality in a favorable way, regardless of whether their gender personality fits a more traditional masculine model or is more divergent (see Herrnson, Lay, and Stokes 2003 for an analysis of this model of campaigns). She Should Run, a 501(c)3 organization founded in 2011 to expand the talent pool of women running for office, began recruiting women in 2018 with the message, "Nominate a woman in your life to run for public office using our #AskAWomanToRun tool and get her started on her own unique journey to public office!" The language they use to recruit women is arguably more friendly to women who may not believe that their experiences or personal traits qualify them for office. Encouraging women with diverse displays of gender traits, behaviors, and experiences may help build the confidence of those who are less masculine and buttress their sense of qualifications that is a key predictor of progressive ambition.

FOUR

Did They Ask?

Masculine Personality and Candidate Recruitment

With consistency, recruitment is shown to be fundamental to the decision to run for political office for both men and women. For example, in their 2012 report, *Men Rule: The Continued Under-Representation of Women in U.S. Politics,* Jennifer Lawless and Richard Fox find that 67 percent of respondents who were encouraged to run for political office by a political actor go on to consider running. But among individuals who were not encouraged to run, only 33 percent report that they had considered running for office (Lawless and Fox 2012). Thus, recruitment is vital.

Recruitment is especially critical for women. In their study, Sanbonmatsu, Carroll and Walsh (2009) found 24 percent of women reported encouragement as the most important factor in their decision to run, compared to 15 percent of men. Moreover, more than half of the women serving in state legislatures reported that they had not considered running until someone suggested it (Carroll and Sanbonmatsu 2013). However, women are less likely to be recruited by political actors, such as a party leader, or encouraged by nonpolitical actors, such as a work colleague or spouse, than men (Lawless and Fox 2010; Sanbonmatsu 2006; Welch 1978; Windett 2014); in some cases, women were openly discouraged from running (e.g., Crowder-Meyer 2013). To explain recruitment bias, previous scholarship has implicated structural barriers, such as a pipeline problem, suggesting that there are too few women in the political eligibility pools (like business or law professions), where recruiters tend to go searching for potential candidates (Crowder-Meyer and Lauderdale 2014; Welch 1978), or gender bias in party leadership (Butler and Preece 2016). Yet these explanations for the recruitment gap are incomplete.

Building on previous scholarship that identifies differences in men's and women's experiences with recruitment, we propose that variation in contact is mediated by individuals' gender personality. Individuals' gender personality is a precise measure that can aid in pinpointing mechanisms that contribute to recruitment bias more effectively than candidate sex in isolation. As with the previous chapter, we suggest that individuals' psychological variation, captured by gender personality, helps explain who is recruited to run for higher office from eligibility pools, such as local government. We expect that individuals who self-identify as possessing more masculine personality traits will report being recruited to run for political office at higher rates than individuals who possess fewer masculine personality traits, regardless of sex. Our theory is that masculinity is desirable in potential political candidates, and that recruiters are likely to observe and take note of trait and character variations, even if unconsciously, and will be more likely to encourage more masculine individuals than less masculine individuals, given the recruiters' understanding of the political terrain, where masculinity is usually rewarded. Therefore, this explanation is an external route for gender bias in the candidate emergence process, and the link between gender personality and recruitment presumes that individuals' personalities are perceptible.

Our primary dependent variable in this chapter is frequency of recruitment contact. We measure recruitment by asking respondents, "Regardless of your interest in running for higher office, have any of the following ever suggested it to you?" Respondents then selected from eight different options: a friend or acquaintance; a spouse or partner; a family member; a women's organization; an elected official; a coworker or business associate; a nonelected political activist; and someone from a religious place of worship (see appendix for the full survey). Our primary independent variable is individual-level gender personality (see chapter 2). Our results confirm our expectation that a more masculine personality is associated with increased recruitment contact. While we should celebrate our results, which suggest that women who do not identify with traditional gender stereotypes are not necessarily punished, at least at the recruitment stage of candidate emergence, these results indicate a positive relationship between masculine norms and American politics, and suggest that by possessing a masculine personality, women can make inroads. Recognizing the preeminence of masculinity to recruitment contact, especially as more women are recruited to run for office, draws attention to the slow incorporation of femininity in American politics, and allows for greater theoretical development surrounding analysis of the impact women make in politics.

Women, Men, and Recruitment

Previous studies have shown that men and women experience recruitment differently, and that encouragement or discouragement affects a subsequent decision to run for office. In general, these studies found that men are more likely to be recruited to run for office than women (Carroll 1994; Lawless and Fox 2010; Fox and Lawless 2014; Kirkpatrick 1974; Moncrief, Squire, and Jewell 2001; Norris and Lovenduski 1995; Sanbonmatsu 2006; Welch 1978; Windett 2014). This literature traces back to at least the 1970s, when women had far fewer opportunities, and bias against women was visible in many areas of the candidate emergence process (Carroll 1994; Kirkpatrick 1974; Norris and Lovenduski 1995; Welch 1978).

Carroll (1994) found a tendency for women in the 1970s to be recruited, if at all, as "sacrificial lambs" by political parties to run in races the parties did not think were winnable. In these circumstances, parties cared less about women's potential to win, because the party had already given up on winning; these sorts of races were against strong incumbents, or where one party was much less competitive. Parties would recruit women to these races to distract them from getting into competitive races, or into races for open seats (Carroll 1994; Diamond 1977; Niven 1998).

Discussion of this trend has waned over time, and "sacrificial lambs" have given way to a general tendency to seek out women in races where candidates are difficult to find (Sanbonmatsu 2002). However, recruitment to competitive races has coincided with the increased real and perceived viability of women as candidates (see Teele, Kalla, and Rosenbluth 2018; cf. Ono and Burden 2018). More recently, studies on sex differences in recruitment have uncovered more nuance and shown that recruitment is conditioned on other factors, such as the issues most prevalent in an election cycle, individual-level professional experience, and that recruitment tendencies vary by political party (Carroll and Sanbonmatsu 2013; Crowder-Meyer and Cooperman 2018; Moncrief, Squire, and Jewell 2001; Palmer and Simon 2008; Sanbonmatsu 2006). Given this scholarship, many assume sex differences in the recruitment process are diminishing, and that progress is being made. However, our argument is that this progress is rooted in associations with masculinity, and we expect that women (and men) who are encouraged to run are likely to have more masculine personalities. Therefore, women's progress should be interpreted with caution, insofar as the perceived benefit of women's election to political office signals a shift in gender norms.

Masculine Personality and Recruitment

Our theory that individual-level variation in masculine and feminine personality should affect experiences with recruitment stems from past scholarship, which implicates a variety of ways in which gender, not just sex, is an underlying causal factor explaining recruitment variation. Yet previous scholarship on sex differences in recruitment does not go so far as to measure the influence of gender on recruitment, even though their analyses point to gender as playing a role, as we draw out below.

First, studies that consider issue salience effects on recruitment support our theory that masculine and feminine personality should mediate whether an individual is recruited to run for office. While most of this scholarship argues that candidate sex signals issue expertise, and thus male and female candidates' failure and success is related to their sex depending upon the public's issue agenda, we argue that recruiters more precisely connect candidates' masculinity and femininity to issue competence and issue salience. We expect that more masculine candidates will be more likely to be recruited, regardless of their sex, given the relevance of and reverence paid to expertise on masculine issues like the economy and security issues at all levels of government.

Issue salience refers to the specific political issues most relevant during an election. For example, economic issues are a higher priority to voters during presidential election cycles, making these issues more salient when voters evaluate candidates. Depending on various factors such as geographic location, events, and candidates' messages, issue salience varies. Following terrorist attacks, or during times of heightened security threats, for instance, individuals indicate that national security is the most important issue facing their communities (Lawless 2004). In 2002, Gallup polls found almost half of those sampled indicated that war and terrorism was the most important issue facing the country, compared to around 10 percent expressing this sentiment before 2001 (Lawless 2004). Unfortunately for women, when terrorism is more salient, studies find male candidates are preferred (Holman, Merolla, and Zechmeister 2016; Falk and Kenski 2006; Dolan and Lynch 2014). This variation in evaluations of candidate competence on political issues is influenced by gender stereotypes. Female candidates are assumed to possess feminine qualities, such as compassion, and be experts on feminine issues, such as education and health care, whereas male candidates are assumed to possess masculine qualities, such as assertiveness, and be experts on masculine issues, such as terrorism (Huddy and Terkildsen 1993; Kahn 1996; Fox and Oxley 2003; Lawless 2004; Fridkin and Kenney 2009; Holman, Merolla, and Zechmeister 2011; Dolan 2010, 2014). These studies that observe gender stereotypes are the basis to suggest that women and men have advantages or disadvantages in voter perception depending on the issue agenda.

Looking at the relationship between issue salience and recruitment, Palmer and Simon (2008) noted that when more feminine issues, like education and health care, are salient, women have a recruitment advantage, but when economic issues and foreign policy are dominant nationally or in a particular district, men have an advantage. These findings imply that gender is an important condition, and women's association with femininity limits their recruitment. Moreover, their results reinforce what we know about sex and gender stereotypes in American politics, which is that masculine political contexts and issues contribute to negative beliefs about women's capacity to govern and lead (Lawless 2004; Sanbonmatsu 2002; Sanbonmatsu and Dolan 2009). Palmer and Simon (2008), however, did not explicitly consider candidates' gender, and whether it is masculine candidates, not necessarily men, who have an advantage when the context prioritizes masculine issues among recruiters.

The male advantage in recruitment is supported by other scholarship as well. As Lawless (2004, 480) notes, "A clear bias favoring male candidates and elected officials accompanies the war on terror." She continues, "Citizens prefer men's leadership traits and characteristics, deem men more competent at legislating around issues of national security and military crises, and contend that men are superior to women at addressing the new obstacles generated by the events of September 11, 2001" (480). However, our argument is that the preference is for masculine characteristics, not "men's," and in this sense women can essentially trespass by displaying masculine characteristics and behaviors, and in so doing, be seen as competent on broader issues by recruiters.

Second, women's opportunities for recruitment are also mediated by their perceived or actual professional experience, and where their experiences better reflect those of typical men, women are equally or more likely to be recruited. For instance, Carroll and Sanbonmatsu (2013) found that highly qualified women who already hold office at some level and come from occupations traditionally connected to political office are more likely to be recruited to run for higher office than similarly situated men. Additionally, Sanbonmatsu (2006) explained that women who serve as state legislators reported being recruited for the House of Representatives at the same rate as men in the state legislature. Crowder-Meyer (2013) also showed that when parties recruit from traditional political circles the process disadvantages women, because women are less likely to be present in these eligibility pools; however, for women in these pools, their chances are much better than for women who are not. While concerns about women's viability seem to have less of an explicit negative impact on women in contemporary politics than in earlier decades, women's viability is underestimated by elites unless they meet traditional notions of experience (Kunovich and Paxton 2005; Sanbonmatsu 2006). We note that these conventional notions of experience are masculine, and thus the perceived qualifications of women who come from occupations traditionally connected to political office may be rooted in the masculine nature of those professions.

Evidence from Crowder-Meyer (2018) supports the argument that women who emerge from traditional eligibility pools are more similar to men than to women who are "ordinary"—in other words, women who are not in elite professional positions. In her study, Crowder-Meyer looks at differences in political ambition between women from elite eligibility pools compared to more "ordinary" women. Crowder-Meyer proposes that "the maneuvering that enables elites—particularly women—to hold the professional positions from which they have been selected for samples of potential candidates makes them inherently different from most Americans" (4). So, what makes elite women inherently different from ordinary women? Namely, "women in elite professions have already taken on, and in some way managed, the social sanctions that can emerge when women violate traditional gender roles to pursue elite professional positions—like political office" (Wood and Eagly 2012, as cited in Crowder-Meyer 2018, 4). In other words, women who are sought out are those who have already successfully navigated a difficult social context and reached elite professional circles. This even further exacerbates the recruitment gap of women of color, who are less likely to have access to elite professional opportunities than white women, and who face intersectional barriers to their success (Strolovitch 2007; Hughes 2011). In this manner, Crowder-Meyer recognizes that there are gendered behaviors and roles that have likely been adopted by women in traditional eligibility pools. We would anticipate that these roles and behaviors are more masculine. Indeed, as Crowder-Meyer (2018) notes, "the processes through which individuals become elite professionals—and make their way into existing studies of political ambition—diminish gender differences in ambition development" (5). In other words, differences in masculinity and femininity between men and women in traditional eligibility pools are likely very small, as we have shown to be true in our sample of city councilmembers (see chapter 2).

Another way that sex has been shown to contribute to recruitment bias is that men and women respond differently to the invitation once it is extended. Looking at individual-level variation in the effectiveness of recruitment efforts, Butler and Preece (2016) analyze differences between men's and women's skepticism that recruitment efforts will guarantee political and social capital if they do decide to run; women are more skeptical than men. The authors suggest that this skepticism arises from women's past experiences with bias, and partially explains the weaker recruitment effects among women, compared to that among men. We suspect that this skepticism may be related to an individual's gender personality, and that women who possess more feminine personalities are more skeptical, but that women with more masculine personalities are less skeptical. For instance, individuals who identify with a more feminine gender personality are more passive and needing of others' approval. This could translate into more reliance on others for support, and where recruiters are unable to necessarily commit resources or other forms of support immediately, individuals who do not possess masculine personalities may be less likely to be swayed by recruitment efforts. Yet women (and men) with more masculine personalities may be more likely to take risks, and be willing to commit to running for office with minimal initial support. Again, we argue that this study by Bulter and Preece (2016) implicates an independent role for gender and adds to our understanding of the relationship between sex and recruitment.

Additional implications of gender effects are found by Pate and Fox (2018). The authors find gender-laden appeals by recruiters to have differential effects on men and women. Pate and Fox test three recruitment appeals—a leadership message, a qualification message, and a community service message. Most relevant to our theory is that the community service message, which we would argue is a more feminine appeal, closes the political ambition gap, because it reduced men's interest in running for office. Therefore, the feminine appeal attracts women, who tend to identify as more feminine. We would expect that including a measure of respondents' gender personality would produce an even stronger relationship with political ambition, given the recruiter's message. In sum, the reviewed studies find that traditional eligibility pools are the primary means by which recruiters identify possible candidates, and that gender stereotypes about expertise influence contact, as gendered messaging affects individuals' responses to that contact.

Thus, we argue that political recruitment should not only vary by sex but also along the dimension of individuals' gender personality, where those who self-identify with masculine attributes will report more recruitment contact than those who do not. We expect that individuals' gender personality will affect whether they are recruited because recruitment tendencies of political gatekeepers may be affected by their own preferences for masculine candidates. This requires a link between potential candidates' perceived traits and behaviors, which in turn affect reactions to them. We propose that actors in a position to recruit candidates perceive the high (or low) level of masculine personality in an individual and either encourage, discourage, or overlook that individual as a potential candidate for state and national level office.

Our expectations for recruitment behavior run counter to some, but not all, aspects of role congruity theory (Eagly and Karau 2002). Some, but not all, of the major predictions of the theory hold here, so we propose some modifications to the theory as they relate to the process of political recruitment. Role congruity theory argues that prejudice emerges when members of a social group attempt to occupy positions or roles where the stereotypes about the social group are incongruent with attributes that are assumed to be necessary to excel in the particular role. As Eagly and Karau (2002, 574) explain, "When a stereotyped group member and an incongruent social role become joined in the mind of a perceiver, this inconsistency lowers the evaluation of the person as an actual or potential occupant of that role." For women in politics, role congruity theory would expect that insofar as there are prevalent stereotypes about women, and prevalent stereotypes about political leaders, and that these stereotypes do not overlap, women seeking positions of political leadership are likely to face prejudice. This prejudice, applied to women in politics, is manifest in two ways. First, the favorability of women who seek political office is lower than men who seek office, because men are a more congruent social group with political leadership perceptions. Second, evaluations of women's behaviors are lower than men's, even if they fulfill the expectations of the role; this prejudice occurs for behavior that is in sync with the role (political office) because the behavior is out of sync with the stereotypical view of women. Previous work by Rudman et al. (2012) finds that women in political positions who exhibit masculine traits face retribution, especially if they threaten the gendered power structure. Additionally, Teele, Kalla, and Rosenbluth (2018) find that women who fit traditional notions of womanhood (married with children) are perceived as better candidates than women who do not. These studies are examples of how external groups penalize women who do not uphold gender stereotypes.

Applied to political recruitment, role congruity theory would predict that women in general would be less likely to be recruited for political office for a couple of reasons. Based on the descriptive norm that women do not fit the role of a political leader, the reliance on gender stereotypes would bias recruiters against thinking of most women as likely strong political candidates (Eagly and Karau 2002). Political science literature lends some credence to this expectation, as we reviewed. Role congruity theory would also predict that masculine men, but not masculine women, would have an advantage due to the injunctive norms that tend to disadvantage women who move outside their communal role and perform more masculine behaviors.

Our theory is in agreement regarding the descriptive norm expectations of role congruity theory, which presents an overall disadvantage to women in political office as a result of gendered norms. We disagree specifically with the injunctive norm expectation: we show that women who are more masculine have an advantage, not a disadvantage, in the realm of candidate emergence. We agree that women do face a disadvantage as a result of injunctive norms in other areas of life and professional development, but in politics the emphasis on increasing representation overrides the injunctive penalty against masculine women.

Although role congruity theory would anticipate that women perceived as more masculine would be overlooked at the recruitment stage due to their violation of gender norms, we expect that recruiters will not punish women who possess more masculine personalities, and in fact should prefer more masculine women over less masculine women and less masculine men. As we reviewed, our argument is that recruitment bias demonstrated in previous studies was not necessarily directed toward women, but due to the various factors that co-occur with being a woman (consistent with the descriptive norm expectation). Women tend to be less masculine, choose careers separate from traditional recruitment pools, and are perceived by others to have an association with feminine gender roles (Burrell 1994; Carroll and Sanbonmatsu 2013; Dittmar 2015b; Sanbonmatsu 2006).

Therefore, we expect that the goal of recruiters to find the best candidates leads recruiters to not penalize women who possess masculine personalities, and in some cases even to seek out these women who present themselves as the "right kind" of candidate (Sanbonmatsu 2006). As noted, women are recruited equally or more than men within traditional eligibility pools (Crowder-Meyer 2013, 2018; Sanbonmatsu 2006). Thus, we expect gender recruitment bias to penalize feminine individuals, compared to masculine individuals, of both sexes. Political institutions largely reward masculine characteristics and behaviors, which is why it is reasonable to expect political recruitment to also favor candidates who exhibit masculine traits and behaviors. In sum, we do *not* expect women who are masculine to be punished at the recruitment stage.

Instead of a divergent reaction to men, compared to women, who fit the normative masculine role of a candidate, we expect that women and men who are more masculine will be recruited more than those who are less masculine. While there may be an overall bias against women, this bias should disproportionately affect women who possess more feminine personalities, which is inconsistent with the dominant view of political leaders, rather than disadvantaging women overall. Our theory therefore presumes recruiters respond positively to individuals who possess the traits and skills believed to predict success in politics (masculinity) and negatively to individuals do not possess these traits and skills.

Role congruity theory is thus consistent in that the gendered roles of politics play a part in recruitment. The main divergence between our theory and that of previous work is the absence of a clear injunctive role penalty, as women who violate traditional feminine gender traits in favor of more masculine traits should be favored rather than punished in political recruitment. While gender roles still disadvantage women as a whole, we expect that it is less punitive in recruitment scenarios than previous research would suggest.

Analysis: The Effects of Sex and Gender Personality on Recruitment

To assess the impact of gender personality on recruitment contact, we asked our pool of city councilmembers whether they had been encouraged to run for office by someone, and if so, then by whom: a friend or acquaintance; a spouse or partner; a family member; a women's organization; an elected official; a coworker or business associate; a nonelected political activist; and someone from a religious place of worship. The vast majority of respondents reported that they were encouraged by at least one of the above types of people to run for higher office, with a mean of 3.39 different recruitment groups selected (*Mdn* = 3, *SD* = 2.21). City councilmembers occupy a traditional eligibility pool, so it is expected that there should be a fairly high amount of recruitment overall (Lawless and Fox 2010; Carroll and Sanbonmatsu 2013).

Our measure of recruitment is of self-reports rather than an observed measure of how many times individuals have been contacted or encouraged to run. Measuring recruitment based on self-report may have some biases embedded within it. Some people may remember their encouragement better than others, or be more willing to report such encouragement. These tendencies could even be related to other variables. Certain aspects of our masculine personality measure, such as being confident and decisive, could be traits that also increase the tendency to self-report recruitment. Those who are more likely to run for higher office may also have more recently had reason to recall the various people who may have encouraged them in the past. Further research on how recruiters view gender personality, or independent checks of the veracity of recruitment self-reports, would be useful.

On the other hand, self-reports of recruitment are appropriate in an analysis of the role of recruitment to decision-making about running for office. Regardless of the frequency of encouraging contact, if an individual does not recall the recruitment it is unlikely to factor into the decision to run for office. If a more masculine personality makes a person more likely to recall encouragement or perceive it as worthy of reporting on a survey, then that recruitment will likely have more impact. In a way, masculinity could amplify the effect of recruitment if it includes the psychological benefit of making a person more aware of the recruitment they do receive (Butler and Preece 2016). The actual recruitment is an external event, but the memory and use of the experience of recruitment in the decision-making process is a psychological process.

Sex Differences in Recruitment

Before assessing the relationship between gender personality and recruitment, we first assess differences in reported recruitment between men and women. Our bivariate analysis finds women reported being encouraged by an average of 3.7 recruiters, while men reported slightly fewer at 3.2 ($t = 2.50, p < .05$). This difference is small, but does show that women serving as city councilmembers, a group already embedded in traditional political networks and eligibility pools, express a slight recruitment advantage over male city councilmembers, in terms of the number of actors encouraging them to run. Breaking down the types of recruiting actors, women note

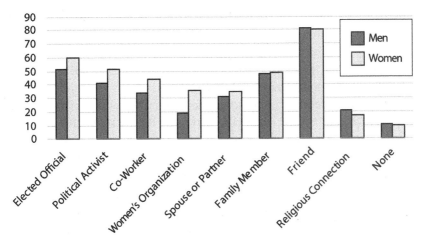

Fig. 4.1. Sex Differences in Recruitment
(*Note:* Each bar indicates the percentage of respondents who reported being encouraged by each type of recruiting actor. There was a significant sex difference (independent samples *t*-test, $p < .05$) for the following actors: Elected Official; Nonelected Political Activist; Coworker; and Women's Organization.)

more encouragement by professional and political actors, but not personal ones (figure 4.1). Women were more likely to report recruitment by an elected official ($\chi^2 = 4.45, p < .05$), a nonelected political actor ($\chi^2 = 5.68, p < .05$), a coworker ($\chi^2 = 6.14, p < .05$), and a women's organization ($\chi^2 = 20.76, p < .001$). Differences between men and women were not significant for reported encouragement by a friend ($\chi^2 = .02, p > .05$), a spouse or partner ($\chi^2 = 1.01, p > .05$), a family member ($\chi^2 = .19, p > .05$), or a religious place of worship ($\chi^2 = 1.37, p > .05$). This lends additional support to the idea that women who run for office (in this case, city council) responded positively to recruitment contact, which as we reviewed, is vital for women's political ambition. Additionally, this suggests that political recruiters in particular are not shying away from female candidates (see Doherty, Dowling, and Miller 2019). However, whether or not women who are contacted by recruiters or encouraged by friends are different from men beyond their sex, like gender personality, is the question at hand.

To assess the relationship between sex, gender personality, and self-reported recruitment contact, we run OLS regressions where our dependent variable is reported recruitment (table 4.1). We present four different models to understand this relationship. Model 1 includes only respondent sex, and masculine and feminine gender personality as predictors. Model 2 adds contextual and demographic control variables for political party affiliation, as well as respondents' perceived qualification for a run for Congress, the perceived competitiveness of local elections in their area, and the perceived competitiveness of congressional elections in their area. We discuss the inclusion of control variables in chapter 2.

Models 3 and 4 include the full model with all control variables, but in Model 3 the dependent variable is a reduced form of the recruitment scale with reported recruitment by women's organizations excluded, to assess whether sex and gender personality have an effect without this category of contact. Model 4 includes only the four political recruiters (elected officials, nonelected political activists, coworkers, and women's organizations), and excludes personal contacts, because recruitment from professionals is

TABLE 4.1. Ordinary Least Squares Regression Predicting Number of Recruiting Actors

Variable	Model 1: Basic Model		Model 2: Full Model		Model 3: Excludes Women's Orgs		Model 4: Only Political Actors	
Dependent Variable: Number of Reported Recruiting Actors								
Gender								
Masculinity	.14	(.02)***	.06	(.02)**	.06	(.02)**	.05	(.01)***
Femininity	.01	(.02)	.03	(.02)	.04	(.02)	.03	(.01)
Sex (Female)	.45	(.20)*	.52	(.27)*	.37	(.24)	.36	(.16)*
Political Context								
Democrat			.62	(.27)*	.62	(.25)*	.36	(.16)*
Republican			.35	(.24)	.44	(.22)*	.15	(.15)
Democratic Woman			-.04	(.36)	-.08	(.33)	.17	(.22)
Qualifications			.64	(.09)***	.58	(.09)***	.35	(.06)***
Local Competitiveness			.14	(.10)	.11	(.09)	.09	(.06)
Congressional Competitiveness			-.07	(.08)	-.05	(.07)	-.04	(.05)
Individual Characteristics								
Income (2011)			.10	(.06)	.08	(.06)	.06	(.05)
Age			-.05	(.01)***	-.05	(.01)***	-.03	(.00)***
Black			.29	(.37)	.28	(.34)	-.02	(.22)
Latino			.09	(.49)	.20	(.45)	-.24	(.30)
Married			.30	(.21)	.28	(.20)	.04	(.13)
Education			-.11	(.12)	-.09	(.107)	-.01	(.07)
(Constant)	-0.27	(.71)	1.49	(.93)	1.89	(.84)*	.08	(.55)
R^2	.07		.27		.26		.26	
N	609		553		553		553	

Note: Unstandardized regression coefficients with standard errors in parentheses. Dependent variable: Models 1 and 2 represents the number of recruiting actors, including all eight types; Model 3 represents the number of recruiting actors for all categories except women's organizations; Model 4 represents only political actors: a women's organization; an elected official; a coworker or business associate; and a nonelected political activist.
*$p < .05$, **$p < .01$, ***$p < .001$

often more persuasive than personal support and to confirm that the political institutions feature gendered dynamics as predicted by our theory (Carroll and Sanbonmatsu 2013). Descriptive statistics for the control variables are presented in chapter 2.

In Models 1, 2, and 4 of table 4.1, sex is positive and significant, indicating that women in our sample report recruitment from more political actors than men. Women reported about .5 more encouraging actors (b = .52, p < .05). This is a positive development, since recruitment is a more important factor in the decision to run for office for women than it is for men, so even a small advantage for women could be important for increasing the number of women who run (Butler and Preece 2016; Carroll and Sanbonmatsu 2013). However, we did not observe sex differences for Model 3, which excludes women's organizations as the source of recruitment contact. The sex variable has a positive effect, as before, but is no longer significant (b = .37, p > .05). This would indicate that the effect of sex on reported recruitment overall is substantially driven by women's advantage among women's organizations specifically. We will further analyze the role of women's organizations in recruitment in isolation below. Additionally, a regression model replicating Model 2 that excludes the role of masculine and feminine personality shows an increased effect of sex, which further supports that what others have attributed to a role of sex differences in perceived recruitment is actually partly explained by the effect of gender personality (b = .58, p < .01, data not shown). Despite the fact that gender personality helps explain some of the sex difference in recruitment between men and women, there is no evidence of an interaction between sex and gender personality in predicting recruitment outcomes under any specification of the model, so we do not include an interaction term in any of our models.

Gender Personality and Recruitment

In addition to the findings related to sex differences, we find a positive and significant relationship between masculine personality and reported recruitment contact in all four models (table 4.1). In Model 1, masculine personality has a positive effect on the amount of recruitment contact (b = .12, p < .001). Moving from the least agreement to the most agreement on a single item on the masculine personality scale predicts a .48 increase in the number of recruitment actors encouraging an individual to run for office. The predicted effect of the greatest shift in masculine personality—

moving from the minimum score of 4 to the maximum of 32—is that the respondent would note contact by 3.4 additional encouraging voices.

Model 2 assesses this same relationship between masculine personality and recruitment contact, but controls for contextual and demographic variables. In this model, the masculine personality coefficient is smaller, but remains a statistically significant predictor of reported recruitment contact ($b = .06$, $p < .01$). Once control variables are included, a one unit increase on the masculine personality scale predicts a .06 increase in the number of reported recruiting actors, leading to a maximum effect of 1.7 recruiting actors. This is a substantively important effect. The magnitude of the effect is more than three times the effect of candidate sex, after accounting for the scale of the variables.

Of the contextual variables, party (specifically identifying as a Democrat over an Independent) and perceived qualification also have significant positive effects on the amount of recruitment contact reported. As explained in the last chapter, recruitment and qualifications are strongly related to one another. We are not making any clear indication of the direction of that relationship, as the two are mutually reinforcing.

Models 3 and 4 present further tests by examining the effect of masculine personality on two different specifications of the recruitment scale. When recruitment is measured as the sum of reported encouragement from all types of recruiters except women's organizations (Model 3 in table 4.1), the effect of masculine personality is about the same as when women's organizations are included ($b = .06$, $p < .01$). This indicates that including contact from women's organizations does not reduce the impact of masculine personality. However, sex is no longer a significant predictor of recruitment. In Model 4, we only consider recruitment by political actors (therefore excluding coworkers, friends, spouse, and so forth); in this model, masculine personality again exerts a positive, significant effect on reported recruitment ($b = .05$, $p < .001$). In each specification, there is a clear and consistent effect from the councilmembers' masculine personality on self-reported recruitment.

Our results find that in addition to the importance of sex, a more masculine gender personality exerts an independent and consequential effect on reported recruitment contact for the city councilmembers for all recruitment actor specifications. Even as women report recruitment from more actors than men, there is a corresponding benefit to being masculine, contradictory to the expectations of role congruity theory, which would expect women who defy gender roles to be punished. We show that people who possess more masculine personalities report being rewarded, in that they are more likely to report that they were encouraged by others, with no clear ceiling of the effect for either men or women.[1]

This explanation may yet be an oversimplification of a more nuanced story, however, especially concerning the effects of feminine personality, and whether women are punished on account of other aspects of femininity. In other words, there may be more subtle ways in which femininity matters for women that are not apparent by measuring their gendered personality traits. Appearance, for instance, may still be a crucial predictor of recruitment for women that is more consistent with the need to overcome a double bind to reach high-level political success. Along these same lines, an effort to shape one's outward gendered behavior as part of a strategy to navigate the gendered norms of society may also overcome any disadvantages seen here in the effect of internalized traits (e.g., Banwart and McKinney 2005; Dittmar 2015b). Although our analysis advances the incorporation of gender more fully into the study of political recruitment and recruitment bias, it is limited by measuring only self-reported traits and not other ways in which gender (perceptions of masculinity and femininity) may matter. In particular, qualitative assessments of ways in which gender is performed and how recruiters react to expressions of gender would further our understanding of these effects. For instance, Teele, Kalla, and Rosenbluth (2018) finds married candidates with children to be more favorable than unmarried candidates without children, thus identifying a double bind that women still face, given that these qualifications place a greater burden on politically ambitious women, compared to men. Our results are merely one interpretation of how bucking gender norms facilitates candidate recruitment. But we do find support for the theory that perceived gender personality is an important variable in understanding supply-side factors in American politics, by incorporating a measure of gender personality.

---

1. There may also be a corollary effect where people who are more masculine are seeking out interactions with recruiters, as well as remembering and focusing on the reinforcement of their confidence and willingness to take risks. There is also a chance that masculinity leads people to overestimate the extent of encouragement they have received. Our data is based on self-reports, rather than reports from the recruiters themselves, so the relationship between masculinity and reports of recruitment could be exaggerating their actual experiences. We have no control for this type of bias. In terms of looking at recruitment as an element of the process of deciding to run for office, the subjective memory of recruitment should be the aspect that affects the ultimate decision. Therefore, this data may reflect this personal bias.

Gendered Recruitment of Women's Organizations

Given that the women and politics literature focuses specifically on the role of women's organizations as a key source of encouragement and support for female candidates (Lawless and Fox 2010; Carroll 1994; Crowder-Meyer and Cooperman 2018), we next analyze recruitment by women's organizations in isolation from other recruitment actors. Consistent with our theory, we expect that women's groups would seek out and encourage masculine people as potential candidates in addition to their general favorability toward women. Hence, those who are more masculine should be more likely to report that they were encouraged by a women's organization than those who are less masculine. Women's groups have a unique place in the field of recruiters in that they are most aware of the gendered aspects of the process of running for office. Therefore, they are aware of the masculine nature of political office and likely seek out candidates that best fit the gendered role of politics.

There are some indications that women's organizations are thinking in terms of gender when seeking and training candidates. For instance, a training brochure from the Barbara Lee Family Foundation (2004, 24) advises candidates: "Voters want to see a candidate who is fearless, yet not overtly aggressive—someone who can make the tough decisions quickly and coolly." Perhaps more than other actors, women's organizations are aware of the biases that transcend sex and are more familiar with the reasons why women are seen as weaker in politics. If so, they may be more aware of the types of women (and men) who would best fit the masculine role of a candidate, regardless of sex. While women are the primary focus of the most prominent women's groups, both men and women reported being recruited by women's groups, so this prediction does apply to both men and women.

Our data show that women's organizations do recruit candidates who are more likely to self-identify with masculine traits. Table 4.2 presents results from a binary logistic regression analyzing the effect of masculine personality, sex, and a set of control variables on the likelihood of reporting encouragement by a women's organization. The dependent variable here is dichotomous, where 1 is yes an individual said they were encouraged by a women's organization, and 0 is no.

Masculine personality exhibits a positive influence on the likelihood of reporting being recruited by a women's organization, after controlling for the effect of sex. In other words, women's organizations, in addition to their emphasis on women, also give more encouragement to those who see themselves as masculine, according to self-reports ($b = .07, p < .01$). While the relationship between femininity and recruitment by a women's organization is also slightly positive, it is not as strong, and is not significant ($b = .03, p > .05$). Despite prevalent effects of both sex and masculine personality, there is no evidence of an interaction between the two variables on recruitment from women's groups or on recruitment overall, and thus we do not include an interaction term in the regression model.

Looking at only the women in the sample (column 2), who are the main target of recruitment by women's organizations, masculine personality exerts a stronger effect than for the full sample ($b = .10, p > .05$), but it is only marginally significant due to the drop in the sample size for this analysis ($N = 170$). The persistence of the magnitude of the slope, despite the drop in the significance, lends further support to the theory that women's

TABLE 4.2. Binary Logistic Regression Predicting Recruitment by Women's Organizations

Variable	Recruitment by Women's Organizations			
	All Respondents		Women Only	
Gender				
Masculinity	.07	(.03)**	·.10	(.05)+
Femininity	.03	(.02)	.04	(.05)
Sex (Female)	1.19	(.23)***		
Political Context				
Democrat	.58	(.25)*	−.13	(.56)
Republican	.31	(.13)*	−1.39	(.64)*
Qualifications	.31	(.13)**	.29	(.13)
Local Competitiveness	.28	(.13)*	.17	(.22)
Congressional Competitiveness	−.02	(.11)	.09	(.17)
Individual Characteristics				
Income (2011)	.06	(.08)	.00	(.15)
Age	−.01	(.08)	−.00	(.02)
Black	.04	(.45)	.25	(.76)
Latino	−.80	(.69)	−.70	(.91)
Married	.39	(.29)	.77	(.42)+
Education	−.02	(.16)	−.03	(.29)
(Constant)	−4.77	(1.13)***	−5.44	(2.27)**
Cox and Snell R^2	.11		.13	
N	583		170	

Note: Unstandardized logistic regression coefficients, standard errors in parentheses. Dependent variable represents whether the respondent was recruited by a women's organization.
+$p < .10$, *$p < .05$, **$p < .01$, ***$p < .001$

organizations are taking masculinity into account when recruiting women. Another interesting shift that we observe is that Republicans report significantly less recruitment contact by women's organizations than Independents, an effect that has not emerged in other analyses of recruitment.

Political Parties, Gender, and Recruitment

Next, we turn to an analysis of the relationship between party identification and recruitment contact. Recent scholarship finds variations in recruitment of women by party (e.g., Crowder-Meyer and Lauderdale 2014). Studies find that the Democratic Party encourages women to run for office more than the Republican Party, and has run a much larger percentage of women as candidates, with the gap growing over time at both the federal and state level (Carroll and Sanbonmatsu 2013; Elder 2012; Beitsch 2015). This gap is reflected in the number of Democratic and Republican women elected to office; while only 23.7 percent of Congress was made up of women in 2019, 82.7 percent of those women represented the Democratic Party (CAWP 2019).

This can somewhat be explained by the fact that voters perceive women, in general, to be more liberal than equivalently situated men, and therefore recruiters may see Republican women as less politically fit for conservative districts or constituencies (Huddy and Terkildsen 1993; Carroll and Sanbonmatsu 2013; Thomsen 2017). Additionally, Republican women are more likely to prefer upholding more traditional feminine roles, and therefore may be less likely than Democratic women to seek or think about running for office (Darcy, Welch, and Clark 1994). Lastly, the Democratic Party has more organizations directed toward recruiting and training women to run for office, and their party is more likely to champion women's issues (Crowder-Meyer and Cooperman 2018; Thomsen and Swers 2017). This contributes to the disproportionality in the number of women in the respective party's eligibility pools, with the pool much larger for Democrats than for Republicans (Crowder-Meyer and Lauderdale 2014).

Although a recent wave of conservatism has swept the Republican Party, leading to conservative women putting more emphasis on women's traditional gender roles to reshape conservative issues as women's issues, Deckman (2016) found that Republican Party officials were reluctant to advance these women and issues. In fact, at the elite level, the greater role of the Christian Right within the Republican Party has reduced the number of women in state legislatures overall (Elder 2012). In sum, Democrats do

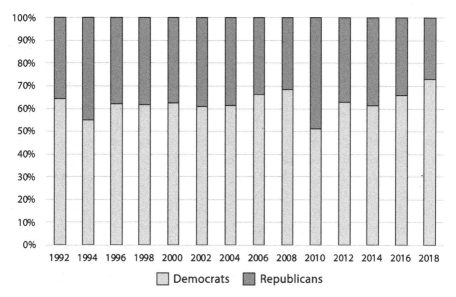

Fig. 4.2. Proportion of Women Running in Congressional Primaries by Political Party
(Data from the Center for American Women in Politics, 2019.)

more, and are better positioned, to actively seek out women, and are consistently more successful at recruiting and supporting women (Crowder-Meyer 2013; Crowder-Meyer and Lauderdale 2014; Crowder-Meyer and Cooperman 2018; Thomsen and Swers 2017). Therefore, this somewhat explains Democrats greater share of women running for office. Figure 4.2 displays the Democratic and Republican share of women who ran in congressional primaries since 1992. For all years, more women ran as Democrats than as Republicans.

To assess the relationship between reported recruitment contact and political party affiliation, candidate sex, and gender personality we use *t*-tests, which allows us to look at group differences between Republicans and Democrats and their recruitment experiences. As was displayed in table 4.1, regression analysis uncovered some effects of party affiliation on the likelihood of reported recruitment. For instance, Democrats reported more recruitment than Independents in all models of table 4.1, and Republicans reported more recruitment than Independents when women's organizations were excluded from the recruitment variable in Model 3. Further, Democrats and Republicans reported more recruitment from women's organizations overall, but, among women, Republicans were recruited by fewer actors than Independents. There are some additional party dynamics visible at work when we zoom in and look at recruitment differences between Democrats and Republicans directly, using t-tests.

Individuals who identified as Democrats report being recruited by the most actors to run for office. On average, those identifying as Independents indicate they were recruited by 2.93 different actors, followed by Republicans ($M = 3.35$), and then Democrats, who report more recruitment contact ($M = 3.62$); the difference between Democrats and Independents is statistically significant ($t = 2.82, p < .01$). Among Democrats, women reported recruitment contact from more actors than men ($M_{women} = 3.90$, $M_{men} = 3.46$, $t = 1.75$, $p < .10$, $N = 296$). Like Democrats, Republican and Independent women also reported that they were contacted by more actors than their male political party peers. However, the difference in the average number of reported contacts with recruitment actors between men and women is smaller and not significant, and the overall number of recruiting actors making contact is less (Republicans: $M_{women} = 3.61$, $M_{men} = 3.27, p > .10, N = 257$; Independents: $M_{women} = 3.28, M_{men} = 2.87, p > .10, N = 111$). This leads us to conclude that the overall advantage in contact with recruitment actors for women observed in table 4.1 is driven by the advantage in recruitment among Democrats more than recruitment among Republicans and Independents.

To assess the relationship between masculine personality and perceived contact with recruiters across political parties, we rely on correlational analysis. Our correlational analysis finds that for all respondents, regardless of party identification, masculine personality and amount of recruitment contact are positively correlated, but this relationship is insignificant among Independents (Democrats $r = .26$, $p < .001$; Republicans $r = .25$, $p < .001$; Independents $r = .13, p > .05$). In sum, the effects of masculine personality on recruitment within each major party largely mirror the results from the regression analysis. Within Democratic circles as much as Republican ones, masculine personality is an advantage to being recruited for higher office by more actors.

Conclusion

Who is most likely to be encouraged to run for office? Numerous studies find men to be more frequently contacted and asked to run for political office (e.g., Fox and Lawless 2010; Crowder-Meyer 2013), with white women, and men and women of color, trailing behind (Juenke and Shah 2016; Lawless 2012). However, women within elite pools do report recruitment contact (Carroll and Sanbonmatsu 2013; Sanbonmatsu 2006; Crowder-Meyer 2013). Moreover, as we detailed in chapter 3, an explosion of women's groups, like She Should Run, Vote, Run Lead, Emerge America, and Get Her Elected, bodes well for women's representation, and over time we expect to see an increase in the number of women in eligibility pools. However, the question driving the analysis in this chapter is whether recruiters, who share the same sorts of bias as the rest of the public, express bias (implicit or explicit) against certain types of women, and if they are recruiting women who are more similar to men (e.g., Crowder-Meyer 2018). In this study, we attempt to answer this question by analyzing potential candidates' gender personality, and whether more masculine individuals report more recruitment contact than less masculine individuals. As we expected, individuals who are more masculine, regardless of sex, are more likely to report recruitment contact. Our results suggest that women's path to recruitment largely still follows the already worn paths forged by men.

In sum, as Dittmar (2015a, 762) put it, increasing the number of women in office in the long run may require "regendering ideal candidates and officeholders." In other words, so long as the perception of the ideal candidate is masculine, women will be at a disadvantage. The analysis presented in this chapter suggests that women can overcome bias, at least at the recruitment stage, yet our findings suggest that their internalized masculine gender personality heavily influences this. Previous research suggested vague references to seeking a certain "type" of candidate, or looking for the "right" kind of women who could be successful in politics. Our study presumes a specifically gendered tone to these types of considerations, where the "right" kind of candidate adopts a more masculine persona and possesses masculine personality traits, such as "confident," "stands up well under pressure," and is "independent." While it makes intuitive sense that these are desirable attributes, that we do not see similar positive recruitment contact for individuals who possess feminine qualities like "helpful to others," "kind," or "warm" is curious. Yet it appears as though there is a lack of encouragement for diverse types of women to run. So long as the women who are more likely to be encouraged to run are similar to men (in terms of gender personality), women's integration into politics will have limited impact on the gendered norms within the institutions and on outside perceptions of viable political leadership.

Further research is needed to examine how conscious the connection is between the personality traits an individual possesses and the subjective interpretation of their personality by both the potential candidates and other actors in roles to recruit. In addition, more research should examine how messages about gender are communicated to potential candidates and how the messages may affect the decision to run within and beyond the recruitment context (e.g., Pate and Fox 2018; Schneider et al. 2016). Lastly, a closer examination of the recruitment strategies and contacts, given the explosion of new groups aimed at targeting women, may uncover more diverse women candidates being recruited.

FIVE

Should I Run?

Masculine Personality and Progressive Ambition

On March 1, 2012, Olympia Snowe, a Republican who had served Maine for 17 years as their senator, published "Why I Am Leaving the Senate" in the *Washington Post* opinion section (Snowe 2012). Snowe's resignation came as a surprise, given her long service to her state and her popularity among her constituency. Why was Snowe leaving? In her own words, Snowe explained that "in a politically diverse nation, only by finding that common ground can we achieve results for the common good. That is not happening today and, frankly, I do not see it happening in the near future."

In general, her resignation was a rebuke of the growing partisanship of her institution (see Thomsen 2017), but more specifically, her letter reflected a deep-seated frustration that she could not do what she had run for office to do: "achieve results." And achieving results is a powerful motivator for women to run for office in the first place (Carroll and Sanbonmatsu 2013). Indeed, as was reflected in her opinion piece, Snowe did not intend to abandon the goals she set out to accomplish, but instead she decided that successfully meeting her goals would not come about from her position in the U.S. Congress. She concludes her piece by saying

if the people of our nation raise their collective voices, we can effect a renewal of the art of legislating—and restore the luster of a Senate that still has the potential of achieving monumental solutions to our nation's most urgent challenges. I look forward to helping the coun-

try raise those voices to support the Senate returning to its deserved
status and stature—but from outside the institution. (Snowe 2012)

The decision by Snowe to resign her Senate seat—and the phrases
she used to articulate that decision—reflect what academic studies have
uncovered surrounding women and the goals they set for their careers. For
example, in general, research shows that women are more likely to pursue
careers that facilitate communal goals, like helping other people and working with others, compared to careers that facilitate individualistic goals,
like accumulating power and gaining personal recognition (Diekman et al.
2010). Insofar as a political career is seen as incompatible with communal
goals, the expectation is that women, who tend to possess communal goals,
will steer clear and the potential for political ambition will be quashed
(see Schneider et al. 2016). This is a theory of *goal congruity* (Diekman and
Steinberg 2013).

In this chapter, we suggest that goal congruity theory—which establishes that individuals will seek out social roles (or careers) that facilitate
their valued goals—provides a framework for thinking about the effects
of gender personality on progressive ambition. In short, individuals who
identify with more masculine traits will be more interested in careers
that facilitate more masculine goals, like a seat in Congress. However, we
recognize that political ambition rarely exists in a vacuum, and although
ambition can develop at any stage in the traditional candidate emergence
process (e.g., Carroll and Sanbonmatsu 2013; Fulton et al. 2006), previous scholarship has shown that crucial to the development of ambition
is recruitment contact or encouragement, and the self-perception that an
individual is qualified to run.

In chapters 3 and 4 we found that individuals who possess more masculine personalities are more likely to develop the necessary confidence
in their qualifications and to report more encouragement from others.
Therefore, in this chapter we develop an indirect model of masculine
personality and progressive ambition, where masculine personality is an
antecedent to perception of qualifications and political recruitment, which
in turn predicts progressive ambition. We anticipate that individuals with
masculine personalities will be more likely to see themselves as qualified to
run and report higher levels of recruitment—and, consequently, respond
positively to that recruitment given their values—leading to the expression
of progressive political ambition. We argue that this is because individuals
with masculine personalities respond positively to each stage in the candidate emergence process, which will lead to progressive ambition. Indeed,

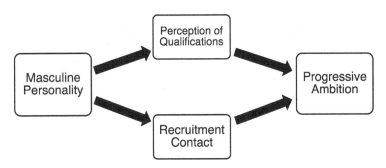

Fig. 5.1. Indirect Model of Masculine Personality and Progressive Ambition

personality traits "structure how individuals respond to various incentives and opportunities related to seeking elective office" (Dynes, Hassell, and Miles 2019, 312). In this manner, masculine personality alone is an insufficient predictor of progressive political ambition. As individuals develop their sense of qualifications, and interact with recruiters or are encouraged to run, their ultimate career goals can come into focus, and if those goals are congruent with a political career, then progressive ambition will develop. We display this indirect model in figure 5.1.

In what follows, we review the foundational and current scholarship on political ambition. While Schlesinger (1966) effectively assumed a level of nascent ambition among all those well suited to run for political office, later research has shown that ambition is not constant, and develops in gendered ways that tend to disadvantage women (Carroll and Sanbonmatsu 2013; Fulton et al. 2006). We then review goal congruity theory, which further implicates a role for gender personality in predicting progressive ambition. Finally, we tie all the threads together to present our theory for an indirect role for gender personality on progressive ambition, via perceptions of qualifications and recruitment. Last, we present the analysis of this relationship.

We show that including a measure of masculine personality as an antecedent to perceptions of qualifications and recruitment experience leads to sex not exerting a significant effect on political ambition. After including a measure of gender personality in addition to perceptions of qualifications and recruitment experience, sex does not have a significant net effect on political ambition. This finding diverges from some other research, but we argue that it exposes gender personality as an underlying mechanism that helps explain sex differences in political ambition. We discuss the importance of progressive ambition as a product of qualifications and recruitment and conclude that successful candidate emergence is the result of a confluence of factors, at the heart of which is masculinity.

Progressive Ambition

What is political ambition? Political ambition is an expression by an individual of his or her desire to run for political office. Political scientists have developed different terms for studying levels of ambition; the two most commonly studied are *nascent* and *progressive* ambition. Nascent ambition refers to an individual's expressed interest in running for political office generally (Fox and Lawless 2005), while progressive ambition is a measure of whether an individual who currently holds office would want to run for a higher office (Schlesinger 1966). Early scholarship on political ambition was focused on progressive ambition because studies typically surveyed state legislators, and scholars were interested in whether and when sitting state legislators would seek a higher office, like serving in Congress, or if they were content to stay put (static ambition) or quit (discrete ambition) (Fowler and McClure 1989; Schlesinger 1966; Fowler 1996). In his foundational scholarship on progressive ambition, Schlesinger (1966) argued that office-seeking is a goal-oriented behavior that is a response to the political opportunity structure; where the political opportunity structure is friendly to seeking higher office, individuals who hold political office at a lower level will seek the higher office. Schlesinger, and scholars who built on his work (e.g., Rohde 1979; Black 1972), presumed that all individuals who already held a political office would seek to move to a higher office, given that a higher office begets a larger salary and more prestige, so long as the opportunity presented itself. In this manner, running for a higher office was a strategic response based on a calculation of costs and benefits. Therefore, this model presumed a similar cost-benefit analysis for all sitting elected officials.

More recent research is critical of this cost-benefit analysis framework, especially studies that consider the gendered nature of ambition. For instance, Shames (2014) finds that women's assessment of the costs and benefits of running for office are not equivalent to men's; women estimate greater costs and perceive fewer benefits than equivalent men. Hawksworth (2003) adds that the perceived costs for women, and men and women of color, are more likely to include concerns about racism and sexism in politics that inhibit their chances relative to white men. Moreover, Carroll (1985) found men and women in elected office to have similar levels of ambition, but women were more likely to forego political opportunities due to family-related conflicts and childbearing (Elder 2004; Thomas 2002).

More formally, Maestas et al. (2006) challenge the assumption that the political opportunity structure alone explains candidate emergence with a two-stage model for understanding progressive ambition. At the first stage is a measure of whether someone is considering running—the formation of ambition. At the second stage is a decision about whether (or when) to run. In this two-stage model, it is possible for individuals to pass up a favorable opportunity, or be denied a favorable opportunity, due to various external or personal factors that would mitigate ambition at the first stage. It is also possible for individuals who lack ambition to take advantage of an opportunity at the second stage and mount a campaign. Indeed, Carroll and Sanbonmatsu (2013) find that women consider the beliefs and reactions, both real and perceived, of other people when deciding whether to run for office—and will take into account how holding office might affect their personal relationships and obligations to other people. Therefore, they find additional evidence that structural opportunity alone does not predict whether women run for higher office, and that additional considerations are necessary for understanding progressive ambition among women. Research on political ambition that analyzes the process through an explicit gendered lens focuses on the social structures that socialize men and women into gender roles, which affect the decision to run for office differently for men and women.

Stepping back from progressive ambition, the development of *nascent* ambition is also more complicated than originally assumed. Scholarship examining the role of sex and the development of political ambition has consistently found a more complex process not only for acting on political ambition but also in developing ambition. As we've reviewed extensively, Lawless and Fox (2010) offer two primary explanations for why women in industries often leading to political careers run for office at much lower rates than equivalently qualified men. First, their research showed that women are recruited at lower rates by political and personal actors (except for women's groups) (Fox and Lawless 2010). Second, they found that women are less likely to think they are qualified to run for office (Fox and Lawless 2011). Taken together, this leads to differences in the likelihood that women, compared to men, will have considered running for office—in other words, will have expressed nascent ambition (Lawless and Fox 2010).

To explain this gap in nascent ambition between men and women, Fox and Lawless (2011) extended their previous work to include an additional, and relevant, "personal background and skill" item. This question asks individuals whether they feel they "have thick enough skin" for politics. Seventy-one percent of men said yes, compared to just 52 percent of women. Moreover, this trait had a significant influence on nascent ambition. From this, we find initial evidence that a gendered trait—thick skin—is a useful proxy for masculine personality that is linked to political ambition. As we reviewed in chapter 3, Fox and Lawless also report multiple messages from women regarding how their belief that they do not have "thick enough skin" makes them believe they are not qualified for political office (see also Kanthak and Woon 2015). We build on these findings by centering masculinity and gender personality to explain why certain individuals successfully navigate the candidate emergence process to hold office, and then develop progressive ambition to run for higher office, and why others do not.

To this ambition research we amend a role for gender personality, and expect variation in political ambition to be affected by masculine personality. As we have reviewed, masculine personality positively predicts both perception of qualification for higher office and recruitment contact. But without congruent goals individuals who are encouraged to run, or believe themselves qualified, may still abstain from running for a higher office. We review this "goal congruity" framework in the next section.

Goal Congruity, Masculine Personality, and Progressive Ambition

The goal congruity framework establishes that individuals will seek out social roles that facilitate their valued goals (Diekman and Steinberg 2013). Therefore, this perspective suggests that alignment should exist between an individual's personal goals and the perception of the opportunities associated with a particular role; when there is alignment, the individual will pursue the role. The goal congruity framework invokes goal dimensions of *communion* and *agency*. Communion and agency are conceptual labels that describe how individuals relate to their social world and represent a framework for studying individuals' goals and roles (Bakan 1966; for a review, see Paulhus and John 1998). Broadly, agency and communion are "meta-concepts," with agency associated with self-advancement and communion associated with promoting the interests of others (Trapnell and Paulhus 2012; Diekman et al. 2017). In the goal congruity framework, individuals can seek to pursue goals related to agency or communion, or both.

Applying this theory to women in politics, Schneider et al. (2016) argue that women are less likely run for office because they seek out communal careers (Diekman et al. 2010), and political careers are not seen as communal. The authors review studies that show political careers facilitate goals related to power, and not necessarily communal outcomes. Indeed, recent scholarship suggests that perceptions of the political environment as necessitating self-promotion, and engagement in conflict and competition, may explain why fewer women want to enter politics (e.g., Kanthak and Woon 2015). For example, Lawless and Fox (2010, 129) report that even among the women "who knowingly possessed the educational, professional, and community experience to run for office," they say that they have the "wrong temperament," "not enough gumption," or are averse to criticism. These responses àre concrete evidence that many women view the political environment as unfriendly to their communal interests and goals. Indeed, when women do run they are more likely to be driven by policy goals (Sanbonmatsu and Carroll 2017) or social goals (Deckman 2004) than by feelings of career advancement. Additionally, the growing partisanship in state and national legislatures may quash the belief that running for political office is how to accomplish policy outcomes (Thomsen 2017).

If (masculine) power goals are more pervasive in political careers, then a theory of goal congruity would predict that more masculine individuals would be more likely to develop ambition for a political career. However, ambition is a function of perception of political qualifications and recruitment, and arguably all components are necessary to produce political ambition. Men and women who are more masculine are more likely to perceive themselves as qualified, develop skills and enter into networks of political recruiters, and develop goals congruent with political careers. The culmination of a gendered process of candidate emergence is the development of progressive political ambition.

Indirect and Direct Sources of Progressive Ambition

We propose an indirect model where masculine personality predicts recruitment contact and perceived qualifications, which then predict progressive political ambition. Therefore, our theory accounts for two indirect linkages between masculine personality and ambition—one, through the perception that one is qualified to run for high-level political office, and two, through recruitment by personal and political actors to run for office.

The first route toward progressive ambition is an internal, psychological causal mechanism, where gender personality traits influence an individual's perception of his or her qualifications as strong or weak, which then affects their interest in pursuing higher office. Previous research has shown that "women are more likely than men to underestimate their qualifications to seek and win elective office. Moreover, women's self-doubts are more likely than men's to keep them from considering a candidacy" (Lawless and Fox 2010, 113). We focus on this gendered basis of their underestimation of skills and self-doubts rather than on sex in isolation. Individuals may feel they are too gentle, not tough enough, or more committed to familial responsibilities to run for higher office, for example. A person may feel that they should not seek the path of higher office due to an incompatibility between their personality, their strengths, and the expectations of political office.

The link between perceived qualification and nascent ambition is clear; those who feel that they are qualified and would succeed at a bid for higher office are more likely to consider doing so (Lawless and Fox 2010, 2012). In running for office, a massive undertaking, a reasonable level of perceived qualification is a justifiable prerequisite. We previously established the link between a masculine gender personality and perceived qualifications (chapter 3). We now turn to the second causal link for progressive political ambition.

The second route of causation operates when others perceive an individual as qualified for office and encourage them to run for office. In our model, we expect individuals who are too stereotypically feminine or not masculine enough will not be encouraged to pursue office or will be actively discouraged from doing so. The causal link requires a link between a person's personality and behavior, where one must not only possess feminine or masculine personalities but also exhibit those traits in some form. In this manner, others (recruiters or encouragers) must also perceive these behaviors and react by recruiting a person for office or discouraging them from running.

As we review in chapter 4, studies have linked recruitment to greater ambition to run for office and to moving up in a political career (Carroll and Sanbonmatsu 2013; Fox and Lawless 2010; Niven 1998). Recruitment has been shown to be especially vital to women: "only with the active recruitment of women candidates will women's presence in politics be less anomalous and, therefore, less conducive to gender stereotyping" (Fox and Lawless 2010, 311). In their model of a relationally embedded process of candidate emergence, Carroll and Sanbonmatsu (2013, 44) demonstrate that "ambition and candidacy may arise simultaneously" through effective political recruitment. They argue that recruitment is an important part of the development of political ambition, and for some, especially for women, ambition does not develop without it.

The response to recruitment in the development of ambition is also gendered. Butler and Preece (2016) find that women are more skeptical of recruitment from political elites. They are less confident that expressions of support will lead to more concrete measures of support should they actually run for office. They provide two plausible reasons why women would react differently to recruitment contact:

> First, women's position at the periphery of professional and political networks may mean that they are simply less familiar with the extent to which party leaders support candidates and the ways in which this happens. . . . Second, women may be as aware as men of the potential benefits that can come from party support during the invisible primary and beyond; however, they may be skeptical that those benefits are likely to accrue to women. This mechanism comes through experience with bias. (Butler and Preece 2016, 844)

Both of these explanations have their root in the masculine norms of political institutions. The perceived bias against women within parties directly links to the ways in which political institutions are masculine (see Duerst-Lahti and Kelly 1995; Hawkesworth 2003). The lack of knowledge of party support structures is also linked to the masculine norms of parties and the historical exclusion of women from positions of power in the party apparatus (Crowder-Meyer 2013; Crowder-Meyer and Cooperman 2018; Deckman 2016; Sanbonmatsu 2006; Thomsen and Swers 2017). For more on the role of parties as they relate to masculine personality and recruitment, see chapter 4.

Both qualifications and external encouragement contribute to the observed outcome—ambition to run for local, state or national-level office. Masculine individuals, compared to those with low levels of masculine traits, will see themselves as more able to be successful in a political career, and will be sought out as a viable potential candidate by family, friends, and political actors. Then, these experiences and self-confidence in their ability will build into a sense of ambition to run for higher office, given a political opportunity. Previous research frequently examined each of these stages in isolation. There is much to be learned from these direct relationships, but we have the advantage of examining the candidate emergence process at multiple related stages through a more complicated and more thorough two-stage process. Our analysis shows that some null relationships, like the bivariate relationship shown below between sex and ambition, can be further explained with an indirect model.

Our central argument is that masculine personality will have an indirect positive effect on progressive ambition through contact with recruiters and perception of qualifications. The argument for an indirect relationship between masculine personality and progressive ambition comes from the role that masculinity has in the culture of politics, but recognizes the necessity of additional factors (qualifications and recruitment) in an actual decision to run. While there may be gendered considerations, like the perceived biases against women in politics or the congruity between agentic goals and a political career, gender personality itself is in the background, not explicit in one's considerations about running for higher office. When they asked directly, Lawless and Fox (2010) found people willing to admit that lack of political skills, lack of a political network, and lack of individual gumption inhibit their ambition. Among those who are candidates and incumbents, Carroll and Sanbonmatsu (2013) discuss skills and individual positive qualities as aspects of why they ran, but not whether the qualities and skills fit with masculine norms. In the decision to run for office itself, we argue that masculine personality is a step removed from conscious consideration. Therefore, it makes sense for the link to be indirect, through the mechanisms of an internal sense of being ready or qualified and an external sense of being well-received by others. Once a person is secure in their qualification and are encouraged, then they develop the intent to run; gender personality helps develop the components of the decision to run, but does not in itself build ambition.

Measurement

We measure progressive ambition with a seven-point scale that captures city councilmembers' depth of intention to run for a higher office. The scale is created by combining the responses to two survey questions, both drawn from Lawless and Fox (2010) and edited to refer to "higher office" instead of "political office." First, the survey asked respondents, "Before today, have you ever thought of running for higher office at the state or national level?" with answer options indicating no, they have not considered it, and three different "yes" options. For those who answer no, our variable codes them as a 0, or never considered running. For those who answered yes in any way, they were asked a more specific follow-up question: "How often do you think about running for higher office?" Respondent options are 1–Many years since considering, 2–Sporadically considered over years, 3–Considered once in the last year, 4–Occasionally consider, 5–Regularly consider, and 6–Currently seeking office. The result is a seven-category variable ranging from 0 (no ambition) to 6 (concurrently pursuing higher office). In table 5.1 we report the distribution of responses along these response options, separating respondents by sex. The mean level of progressive ambition for the full sample is a 1.84 (SD = 1.84) and the median response is a 2, closest to the category "it has been many years since I last thought about it," or a low level of progressive ambition.

The multiple regression models include a number of control variables to account for individual and contextual variables that could affect candidate emergence and progressive ambition, as seen in previous analyses (see chapter 2 for descriptive statistics on each of these variables, and discussion of why each is included). We control for political party with two dummy variables; one Democrat dummy and a Republican dummy, with Independent identification as the baseline. Two contextual variables account for the perceived competitiveness of local and congressional elections. There are also a number of demographic variables in the model. Sex is included in all models to account for the independent role of sex above and beyond masculine and feminine personality. Income is included as a six-category ordinal measure. We control for marital status with a dummy variable for being married or not married. Race is captured with dummy variables for Black and Latino (race and ethnicity are combined in the survey), with white combined with other responses (Asian, Native American, and other, which each only had a few respondents) as the baseline. Education was entered as a scale from less than high school to graduate education. Age is also included, which was recoded from respondents' year of birth to their age in 2012.

An Indirect Model of Sex, Masculine Personality, and Progressive Ambition

There are few differences between the men's and women's progressive ambition. Forty-one percent of the women in our sample said they had never considered running for higher office, compared to 39.7 percent of the men in our sample (t = –.48, p > .05). Therefore, we do not see a meaningful difference between men and women who currently sit in city council seats in this category. More than half of both men and women report some level of progressive ambition, based on our scale. There were no observable sex differences in any category of the variable, which is inconsistent with previous research on this dimension of ambition (see Fox and Lawless 2010;

Lawless 2012), but we survey sitting city councilmembers, whereas these comparison studies survey from the broader population. Women's mean level of ambition is 1.75 and men's mean ambition is 1.89 ($t = -.89, p > .05$; see table 5.1). In sum, when looking only at the bivariate relationship, men and women in this population (sitting city councilmembers) express similar ambition to run for higher office. A multivariate analysis likewise did not reveal any significant relationship between sex and progressive ambition. As shown in table 5.3 below, sex does not affect progressive ambition either directly or indirectly (after summing the indirect effects of qualifications and perceived recruitment).

Turning to gender personality effects, there is no observed direct relationship between masculine personality and progressive ambition. A descriptive difference of means test finds that individuals above the median level of masculine personality express greater progressive ambition on average ($M_{low} = 1.69$, $M_{high} = 1.94$, $t = 1.73, p = .08$), but the difference is not statistically significant; this is displayed in figure 5.2. There is a weak but significant correlation between the two variables ($r = .10, p = .01$). As confirmed in multivariate analysis below, masculine personality exerts a positive yet insignificant direct effect on progressive ambition. Given the observed positive relationship between masculine personality and qualifications and recruitment, this may seem puzzling. However, an indirect model of gendered ambition offers a conclusive piece to this puzzle. As we articulated above, our theory is that there is an indirect causal connection between masculine personality and progressive ambition that operates through the mediators of perceived qualifications and recruitment. As we

TABLE 5.1. Sex Differences in Progressive Ambition

How Often Respondent Has Considered Running	Women	Men	Total
Never considered running	41.4%	39.7%	40.2%
Many years since considering	4.5%	5.4%	5.1%
Sporadically considered over years	24.7%	21.5%	22.4%
Considered once in the last year	6.1%	5.8%	5.9%
Occasionally consider	15.2%	17.4%	16.7%
Regularly consider	6.6%	8.4%	7.8%
Currently seeking office	1.5%	1.9%	1.8%
Total	100%	100%	100%
Mean Ambition	1.75	1.89	1.84
N	198	466	664

Note: Numbers indicate the percentage of respondents that report the level of political ambition. No differences were significant based on Independent Samples *t*-tests.

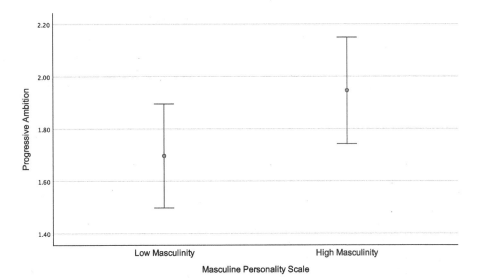

Fig. 5.2. Masculine Personality and Progressive Ambition

(*Note:* Difference in mean "progressive ambition" (scale 0–6) is insignificant across categories of low and high masculinity (scale from 1–32)."Low Masculinity" consists of individuals who score at or below the median (24) on our measure of masculinity (N = 313);"High Masculinity" consists of individuals who score above the median on our measure of masculinity (N = 312).)

demonstrate in chapters 3 and 4, masculine personality has a positive and significant effect on individuals' perceptions that they are qualified to run for office, and whether an individual was encouraged to run for office by an individual or an organization. In table 5.2, we present the summary of those analyses.

We now turn to our analysis demonstrating the indirect effects of masculine personality on progressive ambition, through recruitment contact and perceived qualifications. We find that masculine personality impacts progressive ambition indirectly and through the mediators of qualifications and recruitment. The analysis below tests the indirect relationship between masculine personality and progressive political ambition, with recruitment and perceived qualifications as mediators of the relationship. We use an OLS regression model using the PROCESS program as described by Hayes (2015). In this model, the direct effects of masculine personality on recruitment, qualifications, and progressive ambition are calculated, including controls for the above described covariates. Then, the indirect effect of masculine personality on ambition is calculated using a bootstrapped standard error and confidence interval to calculate the significance of the indirect relationship through each mediator in the model, with the total effect as the combined effect through both mediators. All regression models with masculine personality as the main independent variable in the indirect model are shown in table 5.2.

For comparison, the two leftmost columns in the table repeat the data shown in chapters 3 and 4 with recruitment and qualifications as the dependent variable. The column on the right shows the results of an indirect regression model with progressive ambition as the dependent variable, the same independent variables as the previous models, and recruitment and qualifications included as mediators.

TABLE 5.2. Ordinary Least Squares Regression Models Predicting Recruitment, Qualifications, and Progressive Ambition

Variable	Dependent Variable		
	Qualifications	Recruitment	Progressive Ambition
Indirect Model			
Masculinity (Total Indirect)			.04 (.01)***ᵃ
Masculinity (Through Recruitment)			.02 (.01)***ᵃ
Masculinity (Through Qualifications)			.02 (.01)***ᵃ
Recruitment			.17 (.04)***
Qualifications			.25 (.09)**
Gender			
Masculinity (Direct)	.04 (.01)***	.04 (.02)*	−.03 (.02)
Femininity	−.00 (.01)	.05 (.02)*	.01 (.02)
Sex (Female)	−.27 (.12)***	.44 (.17)*	−.29 (.16)
Political Context			
Democrat	−.02 (.11)	.38 (.24)	.24 (.21)
Republican	−.03 (.10)	.29 (.23)	.22 (.21)
Local Competitiveness	.15 (.04)	.18 (.10)	.06 (.09)
Congressional Competitiveness	−.03 (.04)***	−.10 (.07)	−.03 (.07)
Political Skills	.18 (.02)***	.47 (.05)***	.17 (.05)***
Individual Characteristics			
Income (2011)	.06 (.03)	.11 (.08)	.07 (.06)
Age	−.00 (.00)	−.05 (.01)***	−.03 (.01)***
Black	−.03 (.16)	.49 (.36)	.04 (.31)
Latino	−.16 (.21)	−.01 (.48)	−.31 (.42)
Married	−.03 (.09)	.38 (.21)	−.16 (.19)
Education	.14 (.05)**	−.13 (.11)	−.11 (.10)
(Constant)	.44 (.39)	1.63 (.88)	2.75 (.78)***
R^2	.29	.34	.26
N	540	540	540

Note: Unstandardized regression coefficients with standard errors in parentheses.
ᵃ Bootstrapped standard error based on 5,000 bootstrap samples
*$p < .05$, **$p < .01$, ***$p < .001$

The key analysis of the table shows the effect of masculine personality on ambition, both directly as a predictor and indirectly through the mediators of recruitment and qualifications. The direct effect of masculine personality, indicated in table 5.2 as "Masculinity (direct)," on progressive ambition is insignificant ($b = -.03, p > .05$). After accounting for the indirect effects, as described below, and including our control variables, masculine personality has no direct impact on ambition. Despite a null effect in bivariate analysis, the true effect is captured better by the indirect model.

The indirect effect shows the extent to which masculine personality increases recruitment, which then increases ambition (and the same for perceived qualifications). The indirect relationship is displayed at the top of table 5.2 in three parts (see Hayes 2015). The indirect effect of masculine personality on ambition through recruitment is positive and significant, based on a bootstrapped standard error to calculate significance ($b = .02$, $p < .001$) (Hayes 2015). There is also a significant positive indirect effect of masculine personality on ambition through perceived qualifications ($b = .02, p < .001$). The total indirect effect is calculated by combining the impact of masculine personality on ambition through each mediator and any direct effect to estimate the total impact, which results in approximately the sum of the impact of the components. The total indirect effect is positive and significant, with about half contributed by each mediating variable ($b = .04, p < .001$).

In addition to the effect of masculine personality, the progressive ambition model also demonstrates a remaining significant effect of both recruitment and qualifications on ambition. Greater reported recruitment does show a significant positive effect on ambition ($b = .17, p < .001$). Those who rate themselves as more qualified also report higher levels of ambition ($b = .25, p < .01$). Consistent with previous scholarship, recruitment and an internal sense of being qualified increases the intention to run for higher office. Aside from the main independent variables, only age is significant in predicting progressive ambition. Those who are younger report more progressive ambition. Unlike other research that shows a gender gap in ambition (Fox and Lawless 2010), this analysis showed no significant effect of sex on ambition.

Given the indirect, rather than direct, effect of masculine personality on progressive ambition, we also tested to see whether there is an indirect effect of sex as well. Using the same PROCESS program as above, the main independent variable was changed to be sex, coded as a dummy variable with female as the higher value. For the results, the models predicting recruitment and qualifications are identical to those in table 5.2 above, so only the indirect model predicting ambition is shown.

After including the same control variables in the previous model, men are no more ambitious that women, in either the indirect or direct model. The null results overall, however, are due to sex affecting ambition through recruitment and qualifications in approximately equally sized effects, but in opposite directions. Men perceive themselves as more qualified for Congress, which increases their progressive ambition ($b = -.07$, $p < .05$). But men are less likely to report being recruited for higher office ($b = .08$, $p < .05$). When these effects are combined, it leads to an insignificant total

TABLE 5.3. Ordinary Least Squares Regression Model Predicting Progressive Ambition

Variable	Progressive Ambition	
Indirect Model		
Sex (Female, Total Indirect)	.01	(.05)[a]
Sex (Female, Through Recruitment)	.08	(.04)[*a]
Sex (Female, Through Qualifications)	−.07	(.03)[*a]
Recruitment	.25	(.09)[**]
Qualifications	.17	(.04)[***]
Gender		
Masculinity	−.03	(.02)
Femininity	.01	(.02)
Sex (Female, Direct)	−.29	(.16)
Political Context		
Democrat	.24	(.21)
Republican	.22	(.21)
Local Competitiveness	.06	(.09)
Congressional Competitiveness	−.03	(.07)
Political Skills	.17	(.05)[***]
Individual Characteristics		
Income (2011)	.07	(.06)
Age	−.03	(.01)[***]
Black	.04	(.31)
Latino	−.31	(.42)
Married	−.16	(.19)
Education	−.11	(.10)
(Constant)	2.75	(.78)[***]
R^2	.26	
N	540	

Note: Unstandardized regression coefficients with standard errors in parentheses.
[a] Bootstrapped standard error based on 5,000 bootstrap samples.
$p < .05$, $p < .01$, $p < .001$

indirect effect (b = .01, p > .05). The direct effect is negative, and larger, but also not significant (b = -.29, p > .05). Men have an ambition advantage due to their greater self-perceived qualifications, while women hold an advantage in ambition due to recruitment. Therefore, in our sample men and women are on roughly equal ground in terms of overall ambition. This leaves masculine personality as the more persuasive explanation for observed differences in ambition among those in the city council eligibility pool for high-level political office.

Discussion

Results here indicate that there is a complex process involved in linking gender, in particular masculine personality, to aspects of the candidate emergence process. Masculine personality does not directly predict progressive ambition in this group of city councilmembers. Gender does, however, exert a more subtle, indirect influence on the process by contributing to the underlying aspects of decision-making. The results imply that the decision to run (or not) is not a straightforward effect of masculine personality. However, masculine personality is positively related to feeling competent and supported in the process that leads to the decision to pursue a career in public office. When individuals possess a more masculine personality they are likely to move from one stage of the path to another, resulting in higher political aspirations.

The role of gender personality is crucial at certain crossroads in the candidate emergence process beyond any effect of sex. Although we observed that women in city council seats were recruited more than their male counterparts, there is a corresponding benefit to possessing a masculine personality at the recruitment stage—both masculine men and women are more likely to indicate they were encouraged to run than were less masculine men and women. Previous research suggested typically vague references to seeking a certain "type" of candidate or looking for the "right" kind of women who could be successful in politics. Our findings point to a possible gender personality element to these types of considerations. Masculine personality goes far in helping to explain why women are disadvantaged in the early stages of the candidate emergence process.

The lack of a direct effect of masculine personality on ambition indicates that the focus in looking at the role of masculine personality in the candidate emergence process is appropriate at the early stages of the decision-making process. Research looking at high school students (Fox and Lawless 2014; Shames 2017) would benefit from expanding measures and interpretations of gender to consider more outcome variables, in order to tap into the more subtle ways gender and in particular masculine personality affects ambition. Moreover, beyond the candidate emergence process, incorporating masculine personality into other studies of ambition could lead to better understanding of the extent and limits of the impact of masculine personality on the process of becoming a viable political candidate for high-level office.

Further research is needed to examine how consciously gender personality is embodied by a candidate and perceived by outsiders, and how it is subjectively interpreted by both the potential candidates and actors in roles to recruit. For instance, how does gender personality help predict individuals' goals and perceptions of institutional biases? In addition, studies should examine how messages about gender are communicated to potential candidates and how they interact with personality to affect the decision to run. Our analysis suggests that even as women become more integrated into politics, the inclusion of more women may not have an effect on the gendered norms within the institutions if the women who fill these seats remain homogenous in their maintenance of a masculine ethos.

Throughout the book, we have emphasized the importance of finding new ways to tap into gender beyond the binary variable of sex. It may also be necessary to look beyond the typical candidate emergence process, such as a set of related stages from the development of skills and qualifications, to recruitment, and to the decision to run for office. One further extension of this study would be to look at candidate emergence within a panel design, where the development of ambition can be traced over time, and across variables.

SIX

The Masculine Advantage in Candidate Emergence

Causes and Consequences

The 2018 midterm election was a historic year for women. A surge of women running for office in 2018 led to record numbers of women nominees. In House races, 237 women were nominated to run, compared to the previous record of 167 in 2016. For the Senate, 23 women ran; the previous high was 18 in 2012. Women also broke records for gubernatorial contests—44 percent of races featured a woman (CAWP 2018). This progress has been broadly celebrated both for the symbolic change it signals and the potential substantive change it could usher in.

Inevitably, the conversation has turned to what factors contributed to this wave of women, and growing academic work is attempting to identify and measure the source of the surge. But any efforts to study this phenomenon will be incomplete without a full recognition of the gendered political landscape and attention to how individual-level differences among women and men influence their capacity to maneuver along a terrain that favors those who are associated with masculinity. While we join with others in celebrating the gradual success of women over time and "The New 'Year of the Woman,'" we expect that much of this progress has been made by working within the masculine norms of politics, and therefore may in fact perpetuate the inequalities that have contributed to women's underrepresentation historically. Regardless of sex, those vying for political power in the United States benefit from associations with masculinity. It is this

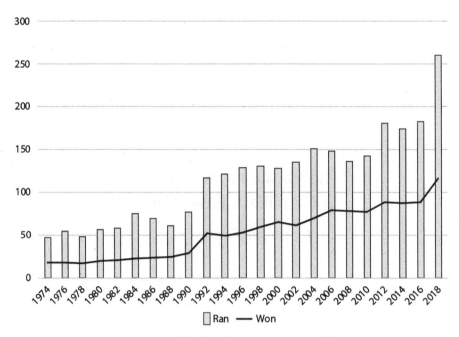

Fig. 6.1. Congressional Races, 1974–2018: Women Running and Winning
(Data from Center for American Women and Politics.)

masculine advantage that has been the focus of this book. We have argued for a conceptual broadening of theoretical and empirical scholarship on underrepresentation to better account for gender—masculinity and femininity—to explain the existing gender power structures and whom they benefit.

In this final chapter, we briefly review our theory and findings. We then problematize this masculinity advantage our analysis uncovers. What do our results mean for broader incorporation of excluded groups? What are the policy implications? What is an appropriate amount of responsibility for the men and women who run for office to shoulder? How else can we bring about more comprehensive change?

A Gender Personality Theory of Candidate Emergence

Considerable scholarship has sought to explain the now pedestrian observation that in election after election, women lag behind men in holding elected office and leadership positions within American political institutions. Even as women broke records in the 2018 primaries, they now make up just one-quarter of congressional membership. As we have reviewed, socialization has been shown to contribute to women's underrepresentation. For example, women are socialized to be less engaged with politics (e.g., Fox and Lawless 2014); women are election averse (e.g., Kanthak and Woon 2015); and marital and parental obligations prevent many women from committing to a political career (e.g., Carroll and Sanbonmatsu 2013; Fulton et al. 2006). Moreover, long-standing beliefs about gender roles influence voters' support for women as candidates (Dolan 2010; Schneider and Bos 2014; Bauer 2017), and can explain the under-recruitment of women for office. Taken together, men have an advantage on these dimensions of perception of qualifications and recruitment. However, looking at differences between men and women means that individual-level gender differences among men and women have been largely overlooked. In particular, does the development of a masculine personality by both men and women give them an advantage in the candidate emergence process?

As we describe in chapter 1, we are interested in whether women's success in American government is closely tied to their compatibility with the masculine norms of American politics (Duerst-Lahti and Kelly 1995; Koenig et al. 2011). It is our suspicion that much of women's progress in the realm of politics and government is because of their adherence to masculine norms, and not to their rejection of them.

Although there are a number of ways to assess this thesis, our argument is that one important source of women's underrepresentation is bound up with social psychology, and, in particular, with gender personality. Therefore, we approach this question of a masculine advantage by developing a theory of gender personality adoption and effects. In brief, we expected that individuals who identify as less masculine will be less likely to run for office, and more masculine individuals will be more likely to run for office. However, the process of converting masculinity into a run for political office necessitates intermediary steps—the perception that one is qualified to run, and encouragement from others to run. To the casual observer, this relationship manifests as more men running for office. However, we observe an internal and external route to power that is fueled by masculinity; more masculine individuals see the political environment as one where they can thrive and that meets their professional goals (internal route), and these individuals are being tapped to run for office (external route). Importantly, the effects of masculine routes to power are accessible by people of any sex.

To assess our theory that masculine personality is positively related to perception of qualifications for political office, associated with greater recruitment contact, and indirectly associated with greater progressive ambition, we administered a survey to 679 city councilmembers from around the United States (30.3 percent women and 69.7 percent men); we describe our sample in more detail in chapter 2. The survey included a gender personality questionnaire, the Personality Attributes Questionnaire developed by Spence, Helmreich, and Stapp (1975), which measures masculine and feminine personality traits. Masculine individuals identify as "active," "confident," and "independent," for instance. Facets of femininity include "warm," "kind," and "helpful to others."

In chapter 3 we developed a theory of masculine personality traits and the self-perception of political qualifications. We argued that masculinity will predict self-perceived qualifications and that masculine men and women will perceive of themselves as more qualified for public office than less masculine individuals. Given the congruence between masculine traits and the characteristics that are associated with running for and holding elected office (Schneider and Bos 2014), we hypothesized a positive relationship between these variables. The main regression analysis results are summarized in table 6.1. Individuals who scored at or below the median score on masculine personality had a mean of 2.38 on the 4-point qualification scale, while those above the median had a mean score of 2.86, a small but significant difference. In a multiple regression, an increase of 1 point on the 32-point masculinity scale leads to a .05 increase on the qualification measure ($b = .05, p < .001$). The maximum effect is an increase of 1.4

TABLE 6.1. Summary of Main Multivariate Regression Results with Masculinity and Sex as Independent Variables

Dependent Variable	Predictor Variable			
	Masculinity		Sex (Male)	
Qualifications[a]	.05	(.01)***	.37	(.08)***
Political Skills[a]	.11	(.02)***	.42	(.15)**
Recruitment (all actors)[a]	.06	(.02)**	−.52	(.27)*
Recruitment (Women's Organizations)[b]	.07	(.03)**	−1.19	(.23)***
Progressive Ambition (Direct)[a]	−.03	(.02)	.29	(.16)
Progressive Ambition (Total Indirect)[a]	.04	(.01)***c	.01c	(.05)

[a] OLS regression coefficients, standard errors in parentheses.
[b] Logistic regression coefficients, standard errors in parentheses.
[c] Bootstrapped standard error based on 5,000 bootstrap samples.
*$p < .05$, **$p < .01$, ***$p < .001$

points on the scale moving from the least to most masculine point on the PAQ scale, a change of 35 percent of the possible movement on the scale. In other words, the least masculine person is expected to be more than one category lower than the most masculine, from "somewhat qualified" to "qualified," for instance. In sum, individuals with more masculine personalities are more likely to express self-perceived qualifications to run for Congress.

In chapter 4 we developed a theory of how masculine personality traits affect recruitment contact and encouragement. Previous scholarship on recruitment contact that analyzed differences between men and women strongly implied that the women who were encouraged to run were similar to men, in terms of their professional vocations and experience (Carroll and Sanbonmatsu 2013; Sanbonmatsu 2006; Crowder-Meyer 2013). We expected that by measuring individuals' gender personality we might tap into one way to measure this similarity. We found that masculine individuals are more likely to report higher levels of being recruited to run for higher office. Masculinity exerted an overall strong effect, with a 1-point increase in masculinity (on the 32-point scale) increasing recruitment frequency by .06 on the recruitment scale. Comparing the least and most masculine respondent, the effect on recruitment is an additional 1.7 recruiting actors. Especially given the effect of recruitment on ambition and the candidate emergence process overall, this is a substantively large effect. Further analysis showed that respondents were more likely to report encouragement from women's organizations if they were more masculine, and that partisan recruiters also sought out those who were more masculine. Gender personality is a strong predictor of recruitment across a variety of ways we examined the effect.

In chapter 5 we presented our theory that individuals with more masculine personalities would be more likely to possess agentic goals, which are more congruent with a political career. However, our model of masculine personality and political ambition includes a role for perception of qualifications and political recruitment, where masculine personality is the antecedent, and structures how individuals respond to the opportunity to run for office (see Dynes, Hassell, and Miles 2019). We found more masculine individuals were more ambitious, but only indirectly. Using a mediated OLS regression model, masculine personality did not show a direct effect on progressive ambition. The indirect effect through the mediators of recruitment and perception of qualifications was significant, however. Individuals who reported higher levels of masculinity increased ambition by .02 units on the 7-point ambition scale for every 1 unit increase in masculinity (b = .02, p < .001). Comparing the least to most masculine individuals, there is a difference of .56 units in ambition. For qualification, the effect was of the same magnitude, with a .02 increase in ambition for every 1-unit change in masculinity (b = .02, p < .001). These effects are additive, so the full indirect impact is .04 units for every 1-unit increase in masculinity on the PAQ scale, with an overall effect of 1.12 points on the progressive ambition scale as the maximum expected positive effect of a masculine personality. Put simply, the difference between the least and most masculine respondent in ambition is an increase by about 1 category in the 7 category progressive ambition scale, which is a change from "occasionally" thinking about running to "regularly" considering a run for higher office. We can also speak to the ambition gap between men and women. Once we accounted for the direct and indirect effects of masculinity, as well as the other control variables, sex was not a significant predictor of progressive ambition.

Our main findings for masculine personality are that masculine respondents rate themselves as more qualified to run for Congress, report more political experience and skills, and report more encouragement from personal and political contacts. Thus, as an individual-level attribute, masculine personality is favorable in the candidate emergence process. Feminine personality, on the other hand, shows no consistent positive or negative impact on the process. Femininity, androgyny, and differential effects of sex-typing exist in many areas of personal and professional experiences, but for sitting city councilmembers in the context of candidate emergence, these variables did not influence candidate emergence noticeably. Similarly, we found no evidence of an interaction between masculinity and femininity, or sex and masculinity, in our empirical analysis. Our assertion, then, is that a stronger masculine personality is a positive predictor of key aspects of candidate emergence, with no clear ceiling to the effect. Therefore, we conclude that those who are more masculine, both men and women, are more likely to perceive themselves to be more qualified to run for office, and are more likely to be recruited to run for office. We then show that recruitment and perceptions of qualification predict progressive political ambition, recognizing that at the root of this ambition is masculinity.

The Masculine Personality Advantage: Implications

What are the possible consequences of a candidate emergence process that is an easier road for those with more masculine personalities? Beyond contributing to the explanations for the underrepresentation of women as a group in American politics, our findings speak to the lack of gender diversity of elected officials, among both men and women. Independent of the effect of sex directly, masculine personality affects an individuals' experience during the candidate emergence process, such as the decision to run for office, which limits the range of gender expressions, qualities, and values in office, particularly at high levels. If the masculine barriers to elected office do not change then there will be a continued gap in women willing to run for office, and potential ceiling effects as women enter the political domain if they do not differ substantially from men. This lack of gender diversity also has likely consequences on legislative approaches to public policy problems and the breadth of solutions considered by elected representatives, as well as the deliberative and collaborative nature of doing the work, which has far-reaching effects on the public at large.

Masculinity and Race: An Underexplored Dimension

In addition to masculine norms largely defining political spaces, political spaces are racialized, and therefore people of color encounter an additional barrier when pursing positions of leadership. If, as we argue, masculinity gives individuals a clear advantage in politics, how does this apply to people of color? In looking at the intersection of masculinity and race, much scholarship is centered on men of color and the different barriers men of color face given that the traditional notions of masculinity in American society are largely defined by white, affluent, male norms. For example, Wood, Harris, and Newman (2015) note that traditional notions of masculinity are out of reach for most black men, who are more likely to come from low-income backgrounds and underresourced schools, which limits their access to a quality education and high-paying jobs; these same barriers affect Latino men. In looking at Asian American men and external perceptions, Cheng (1996) finds that Asian men are perceived by their peers as possessing both masculine and feminine traits, but that in general they are seen as incongruent with notions of leadership. In his study, Cheng found white men to have the greatest advantage, followed by white women, in an assessment of which groups' members would make the best leaders.

Overall, there is agreement that spaces that are defined as necessitating masculinity in American politics are most congruent with affluent white men, and therefore not broadly congruent with men overall. Our sample, being largely white, limited our capacity to draw conclusions about how race intersects with gender personality to explain the supply of candidates of color. We included variables accounting for race, but given the small number of nonwhite respondents, we cannot focus on these variables. An analysis that explicitly examines how masculinity affects men and women of color in particular would be an appropriate extension of our work here. Candidate emergence scholarship is increasingly investigating the intersection of sex and race (e.g., Silva and Skulley 2018; Shah, Scott, and Juenke 2019; Sanbonmatsu 2015; Barnes and Holman 2018; Scott 2018), with explicit attention to femininity as well (Frederick 2013, 2014). We encourage this focus, especially in explicitly incorporating masculinity into models focused on race and politics.

Despite this limitation of our study, taken together our results add an important dimension to the explanations for women's underrepresentation in government, and more depth to men's inherent advantage in this realm. What are the implications of these findings? While this masculinity congruence predicts which individuals will have more success navigating the masculine terrain of American politics, and in particular the candidate emergence process, what might our politics be losing, given this gender personality imbalance? For example, what are the public policy consequences of a political environment that privileges individuals in possession of more masculine personalities and undervalues feminine attributes and traits?

Femininity, Personality, and Substantive Representation

Ample scholarship finds women in particular to either be less likely to run for office, or be more likely to put off running until later in life (e.g., Fulton et al. 2006). Our findings add another interpretation to the consequences of women's reluctance to run. We suggest that not only are women reluctant, but women who may bring a different—feminine—perspective, voice, and experience are even less likely to run for office, due to their incongruence with the masculine norms and behaviors of politics. Our findings support our theory that individuals with less masculine personalities are not thinking about running because they do not see their skills and behaviors as congruent with the qualities the job necessitates or the goals the job affords, and neither do others who might be in a position to encourage or recruit them.

Various groups in American society have yet to achieve influence in politics by electing group members to decision-making institutions where they can wield power (Jones-Correa 2005; Verba, Schlozman, and Brady 1995; Wolbrecht and Hero 2005). However, previous research suggests that meeting other benchmarks of political inclusion (like broader political participation by the electorate) can often hinge on elected community members to political office; when members of historically underrepresented groups are in positions of power, political participation among their communities increases (Gay 2002; Tate 2001; Fridkin and Kenney 2014), and they act as more effective advocates for their group's policy interests (Broockman 2013; Juenke and Preuhs 2012; Fraga et al. 2006). Although there is a rich debate surrounding the value of descriptive representation, some of the more powerful arguments in favor of increasing descriptive representation rest on the observation of these substantive effects.

When a member of an underrepresented group runs for, and is elected to, political office, community members who identify with that individual are more likely to be politically informed (Banducci, Donovan, and Karp 2004), participate (Fridkin and Kenney 2014), and trust government (Gay 2002). Moreover, the election of members from historically underrepresented groups translates into substantive representation. And these studies indeed find that women who are elected to legislatures are more likely to sponsor and support issues that impact women (see Frederick and Jenkins 2017 for a review).

For example, Swers (1998) analyzed congressional votes on women's issues and cosponsorship of bills and found that a congressional member's sex exerts an independent and statistically significant effect on voting for women's issues. In terms of bill cosponsorship, Swers (2013) finds that while the growing partisanship in Congress is affecting the degree to which women in Congress are willing to vote across party lines, prochoice Republican women were willing to defect from their party on abortion bills. Similarly, Swers (2005) finds that female legislators are more likely to cosponsor bills concerning women's issues than are their male counterparts. Furthermore, women with more power in Congress, in terms of committee assignments and majority power status, are especially likely to advocate actively for policy initiatives related to women's issues than similarly situated men. Bryant and Hellwege (2019) show that women who are mothers to children 18 or under elected to Congress are more likely to introduce legislation specifically dealing with children's health and welfare than are women in Congress who are not mothers to children 18 or under. Indeed, women who are mothers do face unique hurdles that women who are not mothers may not (Carlin and Winfrey 2009; see Thomas and Bittner 2017 for a review), and therefore have different policy priorities. However, political party allegiances are important, and women are just as partisan as men. For example, Swers (2016) finds that while Democratic women advocate for "women's issues" like social welfare policies and women's rights, Republican women do not.

One possible reason for a lack of variation in bipartisanship may be the lack of variation in gender personality. Masculine women may be just as partisan as masculine men. But less masculine individuals may be crucial to seeking compromise across the aisle, when it most counts. Indeed, according to Lawless, Theriault, and Guthrie (2018), women in the U.S. Congress are no more collegial, or willing to compromise, than men. However, Holman and Mahoney (2018) find women's caucuses do accelerate collaboration in U.S. state legislatures. Certainly women in Congress or local office differ from men in many important ways, as we reviewed, such as sponsoring legislation that affects women (e.g., Swers 2005) and constituency service (Lowande, Richie, and Lauterbach 2019), but our research indicates that more gender diversity, with respect to personalities, is not necessarily accomplished with the addition of more women. Enabling less masculine men and women to emerge as candidates is a possible means of diversifying policy solutions and further broadening political representation.

Exploring the effects of elected officials' personality traits is a fruitful research area. Although certainly institutions constrain elected officials, there is still the potential for variation in legislative priorities, constituency activities and interactions (e.g., "home style"), collegiality with colleagues and the opposing party, and campaign decisions along personality dimensions. We join with others who call for greater attention to the personality attributes of elected officials. As Dynes, Hassell, and Myles (2019, 310) argue, "democratic elections and public service attract certain types of individuals to seek office, which has implications for elite behavior and representation."

Whether or not policy or legislative behavior differences would emerge between elected officials with more feminine or masculine personalities has not yet been studied to our knowledge. But there is scholarship that does assess the prevalence of a feminine leadership style, which suggests some ways going forward to study a feminine approach to policy-making and legislative behavior. Blankenship and Robson (1995) identify the following as feminine style:

1. Basing political judgments on concrete lived experiences;
2. Valuing inclusivity to accomplish goals;
3. Defining "power" as enabling others (power to, instead of power over);
4. Taking a holistic approach to policy formation, considering the long-term consequences of solutions, as well as structural responsibility for problems; and
5. Moving women's issues to the forefront.

Feminine leadership style presents one means of identifying behaviors that might vary along gender personality dimensions. Gender personality also presents an opportunity to identify intraparty gender gaps on issue positions (Barnes and Cassese 2017). We expect a unique impact for representatives who are less masculine, regardless of parental status, sex, or party identification.

Beyond substantive policy effects, representatives with less masculine and more feminine personalities might disrupt the normal approach to policy formation and debate, and therefore could ameliorate the prevalence of gridlock in Congress. Women subtly differ from men in how they operate in Congress, as we reviewed (e.g., Holman and Mahoney 2018; Bryant and Hellwege 2018). Women in Congress spend more time on constituency service and hold regular meetings with constituents (Thomas 1992). Women are more likely to serve on committees that tackle issues like health care and education that are generally of more interest to women, and are more likely to sponsor bills on these topics (Swers 2002). When women serve as the chair of a committee, they resolve conflict differently than men. Women have more collaborative and accommodative leadership styles (Rosenthal 2000). As Rosenthal (2000) aptly points out, masculine behavior has so thoroughly inundated political institutions that these behaviors are viewed as without gender and accepted as institutionalized norms. Given our findings that many women who enter politics are likely to display masculine behaviors and possess more masculine traits, these fairly modest differences in leadership style observed in previous scholarship could be broadened if men and women who fit more feminine personality profiles gained positions of leadership in Congress.

Research on leadership in business has shown a variety of ways in which feminine leadership styles are beneficial to a workplace culture (see Eagly and Karau 2002). Although there is not a consensus that feminine leadership is superior, one lesson from this research is that having a broader set of options in leadership styles benefits executives and is useful at least under certain conditions.

Congress is not exactly a typical workplace; it has a set of traditions and norms that affect behavior in ways that other workplaces do not. But feminine leadership could disrupt some of the norms that reinforce partisanship, hierarchy, seniority, and building power. It would not solve all problems facing Congress, but it would at least expand the set of options in dealing with the existing challenges to the institution. As Kanthak and Woon (2015) aptly argue, "To effectively represent constituents' interests requires legislators to have a variety of strengths, cognitive styles, and interpersonal skills. The diversity of legislatures is therefore central to representation properly understood" (595). To this call for variation and diversity we would add feminine traits and behaviors.

Achieving Gender Equality: Possible Solutions

How can the masculine norms in American politics be disrupted? We suggest several practical changes to recruitment practices, and that an evolution of social norms that contribute to the gendered hierarchy in politics would chip away at the dominance of masculinity, to lead to greater gender diversity in American political institutions.

Party elite rhetoric can affect candidate emergence and voters' willingness to support candidates currently underrepresented (e.g., Karpowitz, Monson, and Preece 2017). One change that could make a difference is for people in positions of power to actively work to recruit and encourage a more diverse group of people to run for office. We have described a set of examples of women who have fit the masculine norms and found political success, as well as the story of Olympia Snowe, who left politics in part due to the hostile environment she faced in Congress (Thomsen 2017). Recruitment has changed in the last 30 years to reduce bias against women and even advantage women in some cases (e.g., Doherty, Dowling, and Miller 2019). Moreover, there has been a recognition that a more feminine approach to recruitment might be necessary to further women's interests in politics (e.g., Butler and Preece 2016; Pate and Fox 2018).

The next iteration of regendering recruitment approaches could be to seek out and encourage people from any sex who are more stereotypically feminine, rather than masculine. There are examples of successful candidates and campaigns running on their more cooperative, nurturing styles. While many of the campaign ads we discuss in this book from the 2018 midterm races were of women running on their masculine bona fides (and there are many more we could discuss), some women are trying to remake the mold. For example, in her article "Trump Won the Rust Belt with Macho: These Women Hope to Win with Change," Anna North describes the success that women around the country were having in 2018 by embracing their experiences as women, and not running from them. Gretchen Whitmer, Michigan gubernatorial candidate, spoke openly on the campaign about her experiences with sexual assault. In a *New York Times* article, "Mom Is Running for Office," Susan Chira describes an ad by Krish Vignarajah, who lost the Democratic primary race for governor in Maryland. In the ad, Vignarajah breastfeeds her child. While breastfeeding, Vignarajah reminds voters that there are no women in their state who hold statewide office. She closes by saying, "They say no man can beat Larry Hogan. Well, I'm no man. I'm a mom. I'm a woman. And I want to be your next governor." The article also mentions Kelda Roys, who also lost a Democratic primary race for governor. Like Vignarajah, Roys also campaigned with an ad where she breastfeeds her child.

These are just several examples of women running for office by embracing womanhood. However, we would caution that womanhood and femininity are not necessarily the same thing, and we recognize that womanhood can also be conveyed without invoking femininity. Similarly, men running for office can buck gender stereotypes. While we reviewed studies that show there still exist some biases against these styles in politics, normalizing not only women who possess feminine traits and skills but also men who possess and express these traits and skills could contribute to the dissolving of gender bias, much as having more women running has reduced bias against women in politics.

Organizations that seek out women to run, including programs that train and fund women, should be at the forefront of this change (Dittmar 2015a; Sanbonmatsu 2015). In chapter 4, our data showed that women's organizations recruit women, but also encourage men and women who rated themselves higher in masculinity more so than individuals who did not. These organizations understand gender dynamics and are key to increasing the presence of women in politics. If they were more cognizant of the ways in which they encourage masculine norms of politics, they could better serve to disrupt them. In training programs, organizations teach women to build useful skills like fundraising and public speaking. They could also use these training sessions to tell women that both feminine and masculine candidates can have political success. A more explicit focus on the value of diverse gender profiles, and an encouragement of this diversity, could help individuals who otherwise see themselves as unqualified. More and more, candidates, media, and voters recognize gendered norms in politics, but rarely is there an effort to undermine long-standing norms. When gender norms are not criticized, the masculine status quo remains.

Another way to challenge the masculine status quo is to reward men in politics who reject the excessive masculinity in politics and elevate more feminine expressions. Men who discuss politics as needing more compromise, less partisanship, and a focus on caring for others rather than winning and power for the sake of power would help to undermine the hierarchy they otherwise benefit from, elevating compassion for others over oppression. By accounting for gender personality rather than sex alone, we can also speak to the possible effects if more feminine men gain positions of power.

Currently, men are rarely the focus in examining issues of gender in Congress. The focus on sex differences masks the opportunity to analyze variation among men on collegiality and bipartisanship. Voters do hold some biases against femininity in their legislators, so it is understandable that men who violate both gender norms for their sex and the gender norms of political power structures are less likely to run for office. That does not mean that there are not a set of highly qualified, potentially valuable men who could serve in Congress but either have not considered it or have been discouraged because of their lack of fit within the gendered norms prominent in national politics. One of President Barack Obama's talents was to speak in a way to unify the public after a tragedy. In these times, he drew on the more feminine quality, compassion. Despite some criticisms of his less masculine style, or appearing "weak" (see Azari 2014), these moments from Obama's term show that femininity can fit with conceptions of politics and power in contemporary America, and even the presidency.

The gendered norms of politics are especially strong, and at times hostile, at the presidential level. As we reviewed in chapter 1, presidential elections are notoriously a contest between different visions of masculinity, and the highly visible nature of presidential races likely has trickle-down effects to candidates in lower races. We do not necessarily advocate for the undoing of the centuries-old association between masculinity and the presidency. Instead, we would advocate for augmenting our collective understanding of the meaning of "presidential" in include positive feminine attributes, like collaboration, compassion, and humility.

The Democratic Party more than the Republican Party is associated with feminine qualities like compassion. How did this association develop? For all presidential elections since 1980, individuals have judged the Democratic nominee to be more compassionate than the Republican nominee (Heldman, Conroy, and Ackerman 2018). Using a cognitive experiment, Winter (2010) found respondents primed to think about the Democratic Party reacted quicker to feminine words, while those primed to think about the Republican Party reacted more quickly to masculine words, though the effect was smaller. Winter concluded that feminine ideas and traits become more accessible, mentally, when individuals are primed to think about the Democratic Party, and ideas about masculinity are more accessible when individuals are primed to think about the Republican Party. To what do we owe these consistent, and distinct, evaluations of the political parties on the basis of character traits and gender associations?

It is likely an evolution of issue ownership (Petrocik 1996; Hayes 2005). For example, given the presumed association between Republicans and national security, and the presumed association between national security and strong leadership, voters presume that Republicans are stronger leaders than Democrats. Additionally, Republican presidents use more masculine language than Democratic presidents in their State of the Union addresses, reinforcing the partisan gender associations (Roberts and Utych 2020). Therefore, one means by which femininity could be better integrated into the presidency would be for a more overt focus on domestic policies and social welfare, in addition to emphasis on strengthening national security and the economy at the presidential level by both parties.

Challenging media coverage that reinforces masculinity in politics as normal would also go a long way toward changing the political terrain to be friendlier to feminine candidates and politicians. A seemingly benign means by which media reinforce masculinity in politics as normal is their use of military, sports, and violent metaphors to explain political races. For example, Burke and Mazzarella (2008) identify gendered metaphors. Male-driven metaphors are those related to activities or pursuits that stem from a traditional male ethos, such as fishing, hunting, fighting, or athletic contests. Women-driven metaphors were those related to "hearth and home," such as cooking, nurturing, or beauty and fashion. Of the stories they sampled, 66 percent included gendered metaphors; of those, 91 percent were male-driven. Indeed, in political contests, physicality and strength metaphors are so well established that they function "enthymematically" and evoke particular thoughts and actions that assume masculine preference (Anderson and Sheeler 2005, 3). So long as media coverage encourages voters to evaluate candidates based on unrealistic standards of masculine leadership, recruiters and parties will seek out individuals who fit into this mold. Moreover, individuals who do not fit into a masculine mold will not pursue a political career, due to the perception that they are not qualified.

As articulated by Wendy Brown (1988) in *Manhood and Politics*, "More than any other kind of human activity, *politics* has historically borne an explicitly masculine identity. It has been more exclusively limited to men than any other realm of endeavor and has been more intensely, self-consciously masculine than most other social practices" (4). This masculine identity of American politics pervades the minds of the electorate and the media discourse surrounding elections, and therefore encourages masculine individuals to run for office. Women are not immune to this reality, and the women who are most likely to emerge as candidates through this model of candidate emergence are those who are more masculine.

Our results suggest that women have worked within masculine parameters to achieve political power and influence. This approach necessitates that women either mimic men to break into politics or are more similar to men psychologically (Carroll and Sanbonmatsu 2013; Crowder-Meyer 2018). Indeed, women can work toward being seen as just as capable as men of being strong, tough, and resolute, and of being as capable as men to handle issues like national security, defense, and economic issues. But fitting into masculine norms of politics further perpetuates women's exclusion, due to the inherent association between women and femininity. As articulated by Cheryl King (1995):

Unfortunately, the conformity of women to these constructs does little to change the nature of gender power. . . . Instead, women's conformity to masculinized norms reinforces gender power relationships rather than weakening them. For if women are capable of and willing to prove their masculinity in the masculine bureaucracy, there is little impetus for criticism and change. (89)

Thus, the measure of success is not the number of women elected to office, but the changes made to the underlying structure that singularly elevates masculinity and dismisses the value of femininity in our politics.

Appendix

Please select the response that you believe best answers the question to the best of your ability. Please follow all directions and take time to fill out the entire questionnaire. You may skip a question at any time. If you have any questions, feel free to call [phone number] and leave a message.

1. What issue do you think is the most important for your city or town right now?

   _____

   _____

2. On what departments or committees do you currently serve in your community?

   _____

   _____

3. In general, how competitive or uncompetitive are elections for local offices in the area where you live?
   __ Very Competitive
   __ Competitive
   __ Somewhat Competitive
   __ Not at All Competitive

4. In general, how competitive or uncompetitive are congressional elections in the area where you live?
__ Very Competitive
__ Competitive
__ Somewhat Competitive
__ Not at All Competitive

5. What **year** did you first enter your current position as city council member? _____

The next questions (6–9) are statements. For these questions, please indicate the extent to which you agree or disagree with the statements by circling the appropriate response.

6. It is just as easy for women to be elected to high-level office as men.
__ Strongly Agree
__ Agree
__ Disagree
__ Strongly Disagree

7. It is easier for those in the middle class to be elected than for the rich.
__ Strongly Agree
__ Agree
__ Disagree
__ Strongly Disagree

8. Within the corporate or business world, it is still more difficult for women to climb the career ladder.
__ Strongly Agree
__ Agree
__ Disagree
__ Strongly Disagree

9. When women run for public office, it is more difficult for them to build support than it is for men.
__ Strongly Agree
__ Agree
__ Disagree
__ Strongly Disagree

10. On a scale from 1 to 10, how attractive do you consider yourself, with 1 being least attractive and 10 being most attractive?
1 2 3 4 5 6 7 8 9 10

11. Which of the following best describes the way you entered your current position?
__ I was appointed to this office
__ I won a district election with a non-partisan ballot
__ I won an at-large election with a partisan ballot
__ I won an at-large election with a non-partisan ballot
__ I won a district election with a partisan ballot
__ I entered office in some other way.

12. Have you ever run for any other political office?
__ Yes
    What year(s)? _____
    What Office? _____
__ No

13. Have you ever held any other political office?
__ Yes
    What year(s)? _____
    What Office? _____
__ No

14. Do you plan to run for re-election to your current position?
__ Definitely Yes
__ Probably Yes
__ Undecided
__ Probably No
__ Definitely No

In the following section, you will be asked some questions about running for "higher office," which here means running for a statewide or national office. Some questions will also refer to running for US Congress.

15. Before today, have you ever thought of running for higher office at the state or national level?
__ Yes, and I have run for one or more of these offices.
__ Yes, it has crossed my mind.

__ Yes, I have seriously considered it.
__ No, I have not thought about it.

If you answered "No, I have not thought about it," skip the questions 14 through 17.

16. How often do you think about running for higher office?
__ I am currently seeking higher office.
__ I regularly consider it.
__ I have considered it occasionally over the last year.
__ About once in the last year.
__ Sporadically, over the years.
__ It has been many years since I last thought of it.

17. Turning to your interest in specific public offices, which office(s) might you ever be interested in running for? (Select all that apply)
__ Mayor
__ School Board
__ Other City or County position
__ State Legislator
__ Statewide Office (i.e. Attorney General)
__ District Attorney or Judge
__ Member of the US House
__ US Senator
__ Governor
__ President

18. If you were to run for one of the following offices, which would you choose first? (Select ONE)
__ State Legislator
__ Statewide Office
__ District Attorney or Judge
__ Member of the US House
__ US Senator
__ Governor
__ President
__ Would not run for higher office

19. Have you ever taken any of the following steps that often precede a run for higher office? (Select all that apply, if any)
___ Discussed running with party leaders or elected officials
___ Discussed running with friends and family
___ Discussed running with community leaders
___ Investigated how to place your name on the ballot
___ Solicited or discussed financial contributions with potential supporters

20. How qualified or unqualified do you feel you are to run for Congress?
___ Very Qualified
___ Qualified
___ Somewhat Qualified
___ Very Unqualified

21. When it comes to your qualifications for higher office, have any of these thoughts crossed your mind prior to today? (Select all that apply)
___ I am the type of person that runs for Congress.
___ I don't have thick enough skin.
___ I worry about how a campaign would affect my family.
___ I am not confident enough.
___ I am not compassionate enough.
___ I am not likeable enough.
___ I am not attractive enough.

22. Regardless of your interest in running for higher office, have any of the following ever suggested it to you? (Select all that apply)
___ A friend or acquaintance
___ An elected official
___ A spouse or partner
___ A co-worker or business associate
___ A family member
___ A non-elected political activist
___ A women's organization
___ Someone from a religious place of worship

23. Have any of the following individuals ever discouraged you or tried to talk you out of running for office, including the one you currently hold? (Select all that apply)
__ A friend or acquaintance
__ An elected official
__ A spouse or partner
__ A co-worker or business associate
__ A family member
__ A non-elected political activist
__ A women's organization
__ Someone from a religious place of worship

24. In thinking about your qualification to run for higher office, do any of the following apply to you? (Select all that apply)
__ I know a lot about public policy issues
__ I have or could raise enough money
__ I am a good public speaker
__ I have relevant professional experience
__ I am a good self-promoter
__ I have connections with the political system

25. Which of the following best describes your attitudes toward feminism?
__ I am a Strong Feminist
__ I am a Feminist
__ I am Not a Feminist
__ I am an Anti-Feminist
__ Not Sure

26. How do you characterize the political leanings of the state where you live?
__ Heavily Democratic
__ Leans Democratic
__ Balanced between Democrats and Republicans
__ Leans Republican
__ Heavily Republican

27. How would you describe your party affiliation?
__ Strong Democrat
__ Leaning Democrat

___ Independent/ No Party
___ Leaning Republican
___ Strong Republican

28. Where would you place *yourself* on a seven-point scale ranging from very liberal to very conservative? Please **circle** the appropriate number
1 2 3 4 5 6 7
very liberal   moderate   very conservative

People vary in terms of personality characteristics. The items below inquire about what kind of person you think you are. Each item consists of a PAIR of characteristics, with a scale from 1 to 5 in between the two extremes. Please choose the number which best describes YOU.

29. Not at all aggressive 1 2 3 4 5 Very aggressive

30. Not at all independent 1 2 3 4 5 Very independent

31. Not at all emotional 1 2 3 4 5 Very emotional

32. Not dominant at all 1 2 3 4 5 Very dominant

33. Very calm in a major crisis 1 2 3 4 5 Very excitable in a major crisis

34. Very passive 1 2 3 4 5 Very active

35. Not at all able to devote self to others 1 2 3 4 5 Completely able to devote self to others

36. Very rough 1 2 3 4 5 Very gentle

37. Not helpful to others 1 2 3 4 5 Very helpful to others

38. Not at all competitive 1 2 3 4 5 Very competitive

39. Very home oriented 1 2 3 4 5 Very worldly

40. Not at all kind   1   2   3   4   5   Very kind

41. Indifferent to others' approval   1   2   3   4   5   Highly needful of others' approval

42. Feelings not easily hurt   1   2   3   4   5   Feelings easily hurt

43. Not at all aware of feelings of others   1   2   3   4   5   Very aware of feelings of others

44. Can make decisions easily   1   2   3   4   5   Has difficulty making decisions

45. Gives up very easily   1   2   3   4   5   Never gives up easily

46. Never cries   1   2   3   4   5   Cries very easily

47. Not at all self-confident   1   2   3   4   5   Very self-confident

48. Feels very inferior   1   2   3   4   5   Feels very superior

49. Not understanding of others   1   2   3   4   5   Very understanding of others

50. Very cold in relations with others   1   2   3   4   5   Very warm in relations with others

51. Very little need for security   1   2   3   4   5   Very strong need for security

52. Stands up poorly under pressure   1   2   3   4   5   Stands up well under pressure

53. Very honest   1   2   3   4   5   Very dishonest

54. Strong leader   1   2   3   4   5   Weak leader

55. Not at all compassionate   1   2   3   4   5   Very compassionate

56. Not at all ambitious   1   2   3   4   5   Very ambitious

57. What characteristics do you think are necessary for a successful candidate for Congress? (Select all that apply)
___ Aggressive
___ Aware of the feelings of others
___ Independent
___ Can make decisions easily
___ Emotional
___ Doesn't give up easily
___ Dominant
___ Self-confident
___ Calm in a major crisis
___ Feels superior
___ Active
___ Understanding of others
___ Devotes self to others
___ Warm in relations with others
___ Gentle
___ Needs security
___ Helpful to others
___ Stands up well under pressure
___ Competitive
___ Honest
___ Worldly
___ Compassionate
___ Kind
___ Strong leader
___ Ambitious
___ Needful of others' approval
___ Feelings not easily hurt
___ Aware of the feelings of others

58. Which of the above traits do you think is MOST important?

_____

59. Which of the traits do you think is SECOND MOST important?

_____

60. Which of the traits is MOST INCOMPATIBLE with running for Congress?

_____

Finally, here are just a few questions about your background.

61. Are you male or female?
__ Male
__ Female

62. In what year were you born? _____

63. What racial or ethnic group(s) best describes you?
__ White
__ Black
__ Native American
__ Asian
__ Hispanic
__ Other

64. What is your highest level of education?
__ Less than high school
__ High school diploma, but no college
__ Some college, but no degree
__ Associates or Bachelor's Degree
__ Law Degree
__ Other Graduate Degree (MA, PhD, MD, MBA, etc.)

65. What is your religious affiliation?
__ Catholic
__ Jewish
__ Protestant or Christian
__ Muslim
__ No religion
__ Some other religion:_____

66. Aside from weddings and funerals, how often do you attend religious services?
__ More than once a week

__ Once a week
__ Once or twice a month
__ A few times a year
__ Seldom
__ Never

67. In what category was your household income for 2011?
__ Under $25,000
__ $25,001-$50,000
__ $50,001-$75,000
__ $75,001-$100,000
__ $100,001-$200,000
__ Over $200,000

68. What is your marital status?
__ Single
__ Married/Civil Union
__ Unmarried, Living as a Couple
__ Separated
__ Divorced
__ Widowed

69. If you are married or live with a partner, which of the follow-
ing statements best describes who accomplishes household tasks
(cleaning, laundry, and cooking)?
__ I am responsible for all household tasks.
__ The division of labor in my household is evenly divided.
__ My partner is responsible for all household tasks.
__ I do more household tasks than my spouse/partner.
__ My spouse/partner does more household tasks than I do.
__ A person other than my partner and I is responsible for house-
hold tasks.
__ Not Applicable/ Do not live with a spouse/partner

70. About how many hours a week do you spend on household tasks?
__ 0–4
__ 5–10
__ 11–20
__ 21–40
__ More than 40

71. How many children (including adult children) do you have?

    1 2 3 4 5 6 or more

72. How many children are presently living with you?

    1 2 3 4 5 6 or more

73. Please list the ages of those children living at home.

_____

In order to preserve your responses as purely anonymous, please answer the following questions. These responses will be used only to link this survey to any future surveys you complete with the same researchers. These questions were devised to uniquely connect your data without divulging your identity.

74. What are the second, third, and fourth letters of your middle name? ___ ___ ___

75. What is the day you were born? M M / ___ ___ / Y Y Y Y

76. What are the second, third, and fourth letters of the city you were born in? ___ ___ ___

References

Alexander, Joyce M., Kathy E. Johnson, and Ken Kelley. 2012. "Longitudinal Analysis of the Relations between Opportunities to Learn about Science and the Development of Interests Related to Science." *Science Education* 96 (5): 763–86.

Alter, Charlotte. 2018. "A Year Ago, They Marched: Now a Record Number of Women Are Running for Office." *Time Magazine*, January 18. http://time.com/5107499/record-number-of-women-are-running-for-office/

American Association of American Women. 2015. "Why So Few? Women in Science, Technology, Engineering, and Mathematics." AAUW: Empowering Women since 1881. https://www.aauw.org/research/why-so-few/

Anderson, Karrin Vasby, and Kristina Horn Sheeler. 2005. *Governing Codes: Gender, Metaphor, and Political Identity.* New York: Lexington Books.

Anzia, Sarah F., and Christopher R. Berry. 2011. "The Jackie (and Jill) Robinson Effect: Why Do Congresswomen Outperform Congressmen?" *American Journal of Political Science* 55 (3): 478–93.

Azari, Julia. 2014. "Is Obama a Tyrant or a Weakling? His Critics Can't Seem to Decide." *Politico.com*, June 8. https://www.politico.com/magazine/story/2014/06/is-obama-a-tyrant-or-a-weakling-107544

Bakan, D. 1966. *The Duality of Human Existence: An Essay on Psychology and Religion.* Chicago: Rand McNally.

Banducci, Susan A., Todd Donovan, and Jeffrey A. Karp. 2004. "Minority Representation, Empowerment, and Participation." *Journal of Politics* 66 (2): 534–56.

Banwart, Mary Christine, and Mitchell S. McKinney. 2005. "A Gendered Influence in Campaign Debates? Analysis of Mixed-Gender United States Senate and Gubernatorial Debates." *Communication Studies* 56 (4): 353–73.

Barbara Lee Foundation. 2004. *Modern Family: How Women Candidates Can Talk about Politics, Parenting, and Their Personal Lives.* blff.org

Barnes, Tiffany D., Regina P. Branton, and Erin C. Cassese. 2017. "A Reexamination of Women's Electoral Success in Open Seat Elections: The Conditioning

Effect of Electoral Competition." *Journal of Women, Politics and Policy* 38 (3): 298–317.

Barnes, Tiffany D., and Erin C. Cassese. 2017. "American Party Women: A Look at the Gender Gap within Parties." *Political Research Quarterly* 70 (1): 127–41.

Barnes, Tiffany D., and Mirya R. Holman. 2018. "Taking Diverse Backgrounds into Account in Studies of Political Ambition and Representation." *Politics, Groups and Identities* 7, no. 4 (November): 829–41. https://doi.org/10.1080/21565503 .2018.1532916

Bauer, Nichole M. 2015a. "Emotional, Sensitive, and Unfit for Office? Gender Stereotype Activation and Support Female Candidates." *Political Psychology* 36 (6): 691–708.

Bauer, Nichole M. 2015b. "Who Stereotypes Female Candidates? Identifying Individual Level Differences in Feminine Stereotype Reliance." *Politics, Groups, and Identities* 3 (1): 94–110.

Bauer, Nichole, M. 2017. "The Effects of Counterstereotypic Gender Strategies on Candidate Evaluations." *Political Psychology* 38: 279–95.

Bauer, Nichole M. 2018a. "Running Local: Gender Stereotyping and Female Candidates in Local Elections." *Urban Affairs Review*, April 30. https://doi. org/10.1177/1078087418770807

Bauer, Nichole M. 2018b. "Untangling the Relationship between Partisanship, Gender Stereotypes, and Support for Female Candidates." *Journal of Women, Politics and Policy* 39 (1): 1–25.

Bauer, Nichole M. 2019. "A Feminine Advantage? Delineating the Effects of Feminine Trait and Issue Messages on Evaluations of Female Candidates." *Politics and Gender*, June 13. https://doi.org/10.1017/S1743923X19000084

Bauer, Nichole M., and Colleen Carpinella. 2018. "Visual Information and Candidate Evaluations: The Influence of Feminine and Masculine Images on Support for Female Candidates." *Political Research Quarterly* 71 (2): 395–407.

Beail, Linda, Lilly J. Goren, and Mary A. McHugh. 2019. "Madame President? Female Candidates, Masculine Norms of Executive Power, and the 2020 Nomination Contest." In *The Making of Presidential Candidates*, edited by Jonathan Bernstein and Casey B. K. Dominguez. Lanham, MD: Rowman and Littlefield.

Beitsch, Rebecca. 2015. "Stalled Progress for Women in State Legislatures." Pew Charitable Trusts, December 8. http://www.pewtrusts.org/en/research-and-analysis/blogs/stateline/2015/12/08/stalled-progress-for-women-in-state-leg islatures

Bem, Sandra Lipsitz. 1974. "The Measurement of Psychological Androgyny." *Journal of Consulting and Clinical Psychology* 42: 155–62.

Bem, Sandra Lipsitz. 1981. *Bem Sex-Role Inventory: Professional Manual*. Palo Alto, CA: Consulting Psychologists Press.

Bem, Sandra Lipsitz. 1993. *The Lenses of Gender: Transforming the Debate on Sexual Inequality*. New Haven: Yale University Press.

Bittner, Amanda, and Elizabeth Goodyear-Grant. 2017. "Sex Isn't Gender: Reforming Concepts and Measurements in the Study of Public Opinion." *Political Behavior* 39: 1019–41.

Black, Gordon S. 1972. "A Theory of Political Ambition: Career Choices and the Role of Structural Incentives." *American Political Science Review* 66 (1): 144–59.

Blankenship, Jane, and Deborah C. Robson. 1995. "A 'Feminine Style' in Women's Political Discourse: An Exploratory Essay." *Communication Quarterly* 43 (3): 353–66.

Branton, Regina, Ashley English, Samantha Pettey, and Tiffany D. Barnes. 2018. "The Impact of Gender and Quality Opposition on the Relative Assessment of Candidate Competency." *Electoral Studies* 54: 35–43.

Bratton, Kathleen A. 2005. "Critical Mass Theory Revisited: The Behavior and Success of Token Women in State Legislatures." *Politics and Gender* 1 (1): 97–125.

Broockman, David E. 2013. "Black Politicians Are More Intrinsically Motivated to Advance Blacks' Interests: A Field Experiment Manipulating Political Incentives." *American Journal of Political Science* 57 (3): 521–36.

Brown, Wendy. 1988. *Manhood and Politics.* Totowa, NJ: Rowman and Littlefield.

Bryant, Lisa A., and Julia Marin Hellwege. 2019. "Working Mothers Represent: How Children Affect the Legislative Agenda of Women in Congress." *American Politics Research* 47 (3): 447–70.

Burke, Cindy, and Sharon R. Mazzarella. 2008. "A Slightly New Shade of Lipstick: Gendered Mediation in Internet News Stories." *Women's Studies in Communication* 31 (3): 395–418.

Burrell, Barbara. 1994. *A Woman's Place Is in the House: Campaigning for Congress in the Feminist Era.* Ann Arbor: University of Michigan Press.

Butler, Daniel M., and Jessica R. Preece. 2016. "Recruitment and Perceptions of Gender Bias in Party Leader Support." *Political Research Quarterly* 69 (4): 842–51.

Butterfield, D. Anthony, and Gary N. Powell. 1981. "Effect of Group Performance, Leader Sex, and Rater Sex on Ratings of Leader Behavior." *Organizational Behavior and Human Performance* 28 (1): 129–41.

Butterfield, D. Anthony, and Gary N. Powell. 2005. "The Psychology of Aspirations to Top Management: Does Gender Identity Matter?" In *Psychology of Gender Identity*, edited by Janice W. Lee, 47–61. New York: Nova Science Publishers.

Bystrom, Dianna G., Mary Christine Banwart, Linda Lee Kaid, and Terry A. Robertson. 2004. *Gender and Candidate Communication.* New York: Routledge.

Cannon, Carl M. 2012. "Romney, Bush, and Newsweek's 'Wimp Factor.'" *Newsweek*, August 2.

Caprara, Gian Vittorio, Shalom Schwartz, Cristina Capanna, Michele Vecchione, and Claudio Barbaranelli. 2006. "Personality and Politics: Values, Traits, and Political Choice." *Political Psychology* 27 (1): 1–28.

Carlin, Diana B., and Kelly L. Winfrey. 2009. "Have You Come a Long Way, Baby? Hillary Clinton, Sarah Palin, and Sexism in 2008 Campaign Coverage." *Communication Studies* 60 (4): 326–43.

Carney, Dana R., John T. Jost, Samuel D. Gosling, and Jeff Potter. 2008. "The Secret Lives of Liberals and Conservatives: Personality Profiles, Interaction Styles, and the Things They Leave Behind." *Political Psychology* 29 (6): 807–40.

Carpinella, Colleen, and Nichole M. Bauer. 2019. "A Visual Analysis of Gender Stereotypes in Campaign Advertising." *Politics, Groups, and Identities*, July 7. https://doi.org/10.1080/21565503.2019.1637353

Carroll, Susan J. 1985. "Political Elites and Sex Differences in Political Ambition: A Reconsideration." *Journal of Politics* 47 (4): 1231–43.

Carroll, Susan J. 1994. *Women as Candidates in American Politics*, 2nd ed. Bloomington: Indiana University Press.

Carroll, Susan J., and Kira Sanbonmatsu. 2013. *More Women Can Run: Gender and Pathways to the State Legislatures*. Oxford: Oxford University Press.

Center for American Women and Politics. 2017. *Fact Sheet: Women in Elected Office, 2017*. cawp.rutgers.edu

Center for American Women and Politics. 2018. *2018 Summary of Women Candidates*. cawp.rutgers.edu

Center for American Women and Politics. 2019. *Current Numbers*. cawp.rutgers.edu/current-numbers

Cheng, Cliff. 1996. "'We Choose Not to Compete': The 'Merit' Discourse in the Selection Process, and Asian and Asian American Men and Their Masculinity." In *Masculinities in Organizations*, edited by C. Cheng, 177–200. Thousand Oaks, CA: Sage.

Choi, Namok. 2004. "A Psychometric Examination of the Personal Attributes Questionnaire." *Journal of Social Psychology* 144 (3): 348–52.

Choi, Namok, and Dale R. Fuqua. 2003. "The Structure of the Bem Sex Role Inventory: A Summary Report of 23 Validation Studies." *Educational and Psychological Measurement* 63 (5): 872–87.

Choi, Namok, Dale R. Fuqua, and Jody L. Newman. 2009. "Exploratory and Confirmatory Studies of the Structure of the Bem Sex Role Inventory Short Form with Two Divergent Samples." *Educational and Psychological Measurement* 69 (4): 696–705.

Clayton, Amanda, and Pär Zetterberg. 2018. "Quota Shocks: Electoral Gender Quotas and Government Spending Priorities Worldwide." *Journal of Politics* 80 (3): 916–32.

Colley, Ann, Gerry Mulhern, John Maltby, and Alex M. Wood. 2009. "The Short Form BSRI: Instrumentality, Expressiveness, and Gender Associations among a United Kingdom Sample." *Personality and Individual Differences* 46: 384–87.

Conroy, Meredith. 2015. *Masculinity, Media, and the American Presidency*. New York: Palgrave Macmillan.

Conroy, Meredith. 2018a. "At Least 123 Women Will Be in the Next Congress: Just 19 Are Republican." FiveThirtyEight, November 16. https://fivethirtyeight.com/features/at-least-123-women-are-headed-to-congress-just-19-are-republicans/

Conroy, Meredith. 2018b. "Strength, Stamina, and Sexism in the 2016 Presidential Race." *Politics and Gender* 14 (1): 116–21.

Conroy, Meredith, Nathaniel Rakich, and Mai Nguyen. 2018. "We Looked at Hundreds of Endorsements: Here's Who Republicans Are Listening To." FiveThirtyEight, September 24. https://fivethirtyeight.com/features/we-looked-at-hundreds-of-endorsements-heres-who-republicans-are-listening-to/

Correll, Shelley J. 2001. "Gender and the Career Choice Process: The Role of Biased Self-Assessments." *American Journal of Sociology* 106 (6): 691–730.

Crowder-Meyer, Melody. 2013. "Gendered Recruitment without Trying: How Local Party Recruiters Affect Women's Representation." *Politics and Gender* 9 (4): 390–413.

Crowder-Meyer, Melody. 2018. "Baker, Bus Driver, Babysitter, *Candidate*? Revealing the Gendered Development of Political Ambition among Ordinary Citizens." *Political Behavior*, September 11. https://doi.org/10.1007/s11109-018-9498-9

Crowder-Meyer, Melody, and Rebecca Cooperman. 2018. "Can't Buy Them Love: How Party Culture among Donors Contributes to the Party Gap in Women's Representation." *Journal of Politics* 80 (4): 1211–24.

Crowder-Meyer, Melody, and Benjamin Lauderdale. 2014. "A Partisan Gap in the Supply of Female Potential Candidates in the United States." *Politics and Research* (April–June): 1–7. https://doi.org/10.1177/2053168014537230

Crowley, Kevin, Maureen A. Callanan, Harriet R. Tenenbaum, and Elizabeth Allen. 2001. "Parents Explain More Often to Boys Than to Girls during Shared Scientific Thinking." *Psychological Science* 12: 258–61.

Cuordileone, K. A. 2005. *Manhood and American Political Culture in the Cold War*. New York: Routledge.

Curran, Michael D., and Katie M. Warber. 2011. "Examining the Factor Structure of the Personality Attributes Questionnaire." *Communication Research Reports* 28 (1): 86–96.

Darcy, R., Susan Welch, and Janet Clark. 1994. *Women, Elections, and Representation*. New York: Longman.

Deckman, Melissa. 2004. "Women Running Locally: How Gender Affects School Board Elections." *PS: Political Science and Politics* 37 (1): 61–62.

Deckman, Melissa. 2016. *Tea Party Women: Mama Grizzlies, Grassroots Leaders, and the Changing Face of the American Right*. New York: New York University Press.

Dery, Mark. 2007. "Wimps, Wussies, and W." *Los Angeles Times*, May 3.

Diamond, Irene. 1977. *Sex Roles in the State House*. New Haven: Yale University Press.

Dicker, Rachel. 2016. "Donald Trump's #LittleMarco Is the Internet's New Favorite Thing." *USNews.com*, March 4. https://www.usnews.com/news/articles/2016-03-04/donald-trump-called-marco-rubio-little-marco-at-the-gop-debate-and-twitter-went-crazy

Diekman, Amanda B., Elizabeth R. Brown, Amanda M. Johnston, and Emily K. Clark. 2010. "Seeking Congruity between Goals and Roles: A New Look at Why Women Opt Out of Science, Technology, Engineering, and Mathematics Careers." *Psychological Science* 21: 1051–57.

Diekman, Amanda B., and Alice H. Eagly. 2000. "Stereotypes as Dynamic Constructs: Women and Men of the Past, Present, and Future." *Personality and Social Psychology Bulletin* 26 (10): 1171–88.

Diekman, Amanda B., and Mia Steinberg. 2013. "Navigating Social Roles in Pursuit of Important Goals: A Communal Goal Congruity Account of STEM Pursuits." *Social and Personality Psychology Compass* 7 (7): 487–501.

Diekman, Amanda B., Mia Steinberg, Elizabeth R. Brown, Aimee L. Belanger, and Emily K. Clark. 2017. "A Goal Congruity Model of Role Entry, Engagement, and Exit: Understanding Communal Goal Processes in STEM Gender Gaps." *Personality and Social Psychology Review* 21 (2): 142–75.

Diekman, Amanda B., Erica S. Weisgram, and Aimee L. Belanger. 2015. "New Routes to Recruiting and Retaining Women in STEM: Policy Implications of a Communal Goal Congruity Perspective." *Social Issues and Policy Review* 9 (1): 52–88.

Dittmar, Kelly. 2015a. "Encouragement Is Not Enough: Addressing Social and Structural Barriers to Female Recruitment." *Politics and Gender* 11 (4): 759–65.

Dittmar, Kelly. 2015b. *Navigating Gendered Terrain: Stereotypes and Strategy in Political Campaigns*. Philadelphia: Temple University Press.

Doherty, David, Conor M. Dowling, and Michael G. Miller. 2019. "Do Party Chairs Think Women and Minority Candidates Can Win? Evidence from a Conjoint Experiment." *Journal of Politics* 81, no. 4. https://doi.org/10.1086/704698

Dolan, Kathleen. 2004. *Voting for Women: How the Public Evaluates Women Candidates*. Boulder, CO: Westview Press.

Dolan, Kathleen. 2010. "The Impact of Gender Stereotyped Evaluations on Support for Women Candidates." *Political Behavior* 32 (1): 69–88.

Dolan, Kathleen. 2014. "Gender Stereotypes, Candidate Evaluations, and Voting for Women Candidates: What Really Matters?" *Political Research Quarterly* 67 (1): 96–107.

Dolan, Kathleen, and Lynne E. Ford. 1995. "Women in the State Legislatures: Feminist Identity and Legislative Behaviors." *American Politics Quarterly* 23 (1): 96–108.

Dolan, Kathleen, and Timothy Lynch. 2014. "It Takes a Survey: Understanding Gender Stereotypes, Abstract Attitudes, and Voting for Women Candidates." *American Politics Research* 42 (4): 656–76.

Donnelly, Kristin, and Jean M. Twenge. 2012. "Masculine and Feminine Traits on the Bem Sex-Role Inventory, 1993–2012: A Cross-Temporal Meta-Analysis." *Sex Roles* 76 (9–10): 556–65.

Duerst-Lahti, Georgia, and Rita Mae Kelly. 1995. *Gender Power, Leadership, and Governance*. Ann Arbor: University of Michigan Press.

Dynes, Adam M., Hans J. G. Hassell, and Matthew R. Miles. 2019. "The Personality of the Political Ambitious." *Political Behavior* 41 (2): 309–36.

Eagly, Alice H., and Steven J. Karau. 2002. "Role Congruity Theory of Prejudice toward Female Leaders." *Psychological Review* 109 (3): 573–98.

Eagly, Alice H., and Wendy Wood. 2017. "Janet Taylor Spence: Innovator in the Study of Gender." *Sex Roles* 77 (11–12): 725–33.

Ebstein, Richard P., Johnathan Benjamin, and Robert H. Belmaker. 2003. "Behavioral Genetics, Genomics, and Personality." In *Behavioral Genetics in the Postgenomic Era*, edited by Robert Plomin, John C. DeFries, Ian W. Craig, and Peter McGuffin, 365–88. Washington, DC: American Psychological Associations.

Elder, Laurel. 2004. "Why Women Don't Run: Explaining Women's Underrepresentation in America's Political Institutions." *Women & Politics* 26 (2): 27–56.

Elder, Laurel. 2012. "The Partisan Gap among Women State Legislators." *Journal of Women, Politics and Policy* 33 (1): 65–85.

Falk, Erica, and Kate Kenski. 2006. "Issue Saliency and Gender Stereotypes: Support for Women as Presidents in Times of War and Terrorism." *Social Science Quarterly* 87 (1): 1–18.

Farris, Emily M., and Mirya R. Holman. 2014. "Social Capital and Solving the Puzzle of Black Women's Political Participation." *Politics, Groups and Identities* 2 (3): 331–49.

Fowler, Linda L. 1996. "Who Runs for Congress?" *PS: Political Science and Politics* 29 (3): 430–34.

Fowler, Linda L., and Robert D. McClure. 1990. *Political Ambition: Who Decides to Run for Congress.* New Haven: Yale University Press.

Fox, Richard L., and Jennifer L. Lawless. 2004. "Entering the Arena? Gender and the Decision to Run for Office." *American Journal of Political Science* 48 (2): 264–80.

Fox, Richard L., and Jennifer L. Lawless. 2005. "To Run or Not to Run for Office: Explaining Nascent Political Ambition." *American Journal of Political Science* 49 (3): 642–59.

Fox, Richard L., and Jennifer L. Lawless. 2010. "If Only They'd Ask: Gender, Recruitment, and Political Ambition." *Journal of Politics* 72 (2): 310–26.

Fox, Richard L., and Jennifer L. Lawless. 2011. "Gendered Perceptions and Political Candidacies: A Central Barrier to Women's Equality in Electoral Politics." *American Journal of Political Science* 55 (1): 59–73.

Fox, Richard L., and Jennifer L. Lawless. 2014. "Uncovering the Origins of the Gender Gap in Political Ambition." *American Political Science Review* 108 (3): 499–519.

Fox, Richard L., and Zoe M. Oxley. 2003. "Gender Stereotyping in State Executive Elections: Candidate Selection and Success," *Journal of Politics* 65 (3): 833–50.

Fraga, Luis Ricardo, Linda Lopez, Valerie Martinez-Ebers, and Ricardo Ramirez. 2006. "Gender and Ethnicity: Patterns of Electoral Success and Legislative Advocacy among Latina and Latino State Officials in Four States." *Journal of Women, Politics, and Policy* 26 (3–4): 121–45.

Frederick, Angela. 2013. "Bringing Narrative In: Race-Gender Storytelling, Political Ambition, and Women's Paths to Public Office." *Journal of Women, Politics, and Policy* 34 (2): 113–37.

Frederick, Angela. 2014. "'Who Better to Do It Than Me!': Race, Gender and the Deciding to Run Accounts of Political Women in Texas." *Quantitative Sociology* 37 (3) 301–21.

Frederick, Brian. 2009. "Are Female House Members Still More Liberal in a Polarized Era? The Conditional Nature of the Relationship between Descriptive and Substantive Representation." *Congress and the Presidency* 36 (2): 181–202.

Frederick, Brian. 2011. "Gender Turnover and Roll Call Voting in the U.S. Senate." *Journal of Women, Politics and Policy* 32 (3): 193–210.

Frederick, Brian, and Shannon Jenkins. 2017. "The Impact of Gender in the Legislative Process." In *The Political Psychology of Women in U.S. Politics*, edited by A. L. Bos and M. C. Schneider. New York: Routledge.

Fridkin, Kim L., and Patrick J. Kenney. 2009. "The Role of Gender Stereotypes in U.S. Senate Campaigns." *Politics and Gender* 5 (3): 301–24.

Fridkin, Kim L., and Patrick J. Kenney. 2014. "How the Gender of U.S. Senators Influences People's Understanding and Engagement in Politics." *Journal of Politics* 76 (4): 1017–31.

Fulton, Sarah A. 2012. "Running Backwards and in High Heels: The Gendered Quality Gap and Incumbent Electoral Success." *Political Research Quarterly* 65 (2): 303–14.

Fulton, Sarah A., Cherie D. Maestas, L. Sandy Maisel, and Walter J. Stone. 2006. "The Sense of a Woman: Gender, Ambition, and the Decision to Run for Congress." *Political Research Quarterly* 59 (2): 235–48.

Gallup. 2019. "In Depth Topics: A to Z: The Presidency." Gallup. https://news.gal lup.com/poll/4729/presidency.aspx

Garber-Paul, Elisabeth. 2016. "Naked Trump Statues: Meet Anarchist Artists Behind 'Emperor Has No Balls.'" *Rolling Stone*, August 19. https://www.roll ingstone.com/culture/culture-features/naked-trump-statues-meet-anarchist-artists-behind-emperor-has-no-balls-249522/

Gay, Claudine. 2002. "Spirals of Trust? The Effect of Descriptive Representation on the Relationship between Citizens and Their Government." *American Journal of Political Science* 46 (4): 717–32.

Geiger, A. W., Kristen Bialik, and John Gramlich. 2019. "The Changing Face of Congress in 6 Charts." *Pew Research Center*, February 15. https://www.pewre search.org/fact-tank/2019/02/15/the-changing-face-of-congress/

Gerber, Alan S., Gregory A. Huber, David Doherty, Conor M. Dowling, and Shang E. Ha. 2010. "Personality and Political Attitudes: Relationships across Issue Domains and Political Contexts." *American Political Science Review* 104 (1): 111–33.

Gerber, Alan S., Gregory A. Huber, David Doherty, Conor M. Dowling, and Costas Panagopoulos. 2013. "Big Five Personality Traits and Responses to Persuasive Appeals: Results from Voter Turnout Experiments." *Political Behavior* 35 (4): 687–728.

Gerrity, Jessica C., Tracy Osborn, and Jeanette Morehouse Mendez. 2007. "Women and Representation: A Different View of the District?" *Politics and Gender* 3 (2): 179–200.

Godbole, Maya A., Noelle A. Malvar, and Virginia V. Valian. 2019. "Gender, Modern Sexism, and the 2016 Election." *Politics, Groups, and Identities* 7, no. 3: 700–712. https://doi.org/10.1080/21565503.2019.1633934

Goodkind, Nicole. 2018. "Pink Wave: Here Are the Records Women Are Breaking in the 2018 Midterm Election Cycle." *Newsweek*, August 8. https://www.news week.com/women-records-2018-midterms-pink-wave-1063758

Gordon, Ann, and Jerry Miller. 2003. "Gender, Race, and the Oval Office." In *Anticipating Madam President*, edited by Robert P. Watson and Ann Gordon. Boulder, CO: Lynne Rienner.

Goren, Lilly J. 2018. "Authenticity and Emotion: Hillary Rodham Clinton's Dual Constraints." *Politics and Gender* 14 (1): 111–15.

Greenlee, Jill. 2014. *The Political Consequences of Motherhood*. Ann Arbor: University of Michigan Press.

Hall, Andrew B. 2019. *Who Wants to Run? How the Devaluing of Political Office Drives Polarization*. Chicago: University of Chicago Press.

Haslett, Cheyenne. 2018. "In Pennsylvania Primary, a Test for 'Pink Wave' with Record Number of Women Running." *ABC News*, May 15.

Hawkesworth, Mary. 2003. "Congressional Enactments of Race-Gender: Toward a Theory of Raced-Gendered Institutions." *American Political Science Review* 97 (4): 529–50.

Hayes, Andrew F. 2015. *Introduction to Mediation, Moderation, and Conditional Process Analysis*. New York: Guilford Press.

Hayes, Danny. 2005. "Candidate Qualities through a Partisan Lens: A Theory of Trait Ownership." *American Journal of Political Science* 49 (4): 908–23.

Hayes, Danny. 2011. "When Gender and Party Collide: Stereotyping in Candidate Trait Attribution." *Politics and Gender* 7 (2): 133–65.

Hayes, Danny, and Jennifer L. Lawless. 2016. *Women on the Run: Gender, Media, and Political Campaigns in a Polarized Era.* New York: Cambridge University Press.

Heith, Diane J. 2003. "The Lipstick Watch: Media Coverage, Gender, and Presidential Campaigns." In *Anticipating Madam President*, edited by Robert P. Watson and Ann Gordon, 123–30. Boulder, CO: Lynne Rienner.

Heldman, Caroline, Meredith Conroy, and Alissa Ackerman. 2018. *Sex, Gender, and the 2016 Presidential Election.* Thousand Oaks, CA: ABC-CLIO.

Helmreich, Robert L., Janet T. Spence, and John A. Wilhelm. 1981. "A Psychometric Analysis of the Personal Attributes Questionnaire." *Sex Roles* 7 (11): 1097–1108.

Herrnson, Paul S., J. Celeste Lay, and Atiya Kai Stokes. 2003. "Women Running 'as Women': Candidate Gender, Campaign Issues, and Voter-Targeting Strategies." *Journal of Politics* 65 (1): 244–55.

Hibbing, Matthew V., Melinda Ritchie, and Mary R. Anderson. 2011. "Personality and Political Discussion." *Political Behavior* 33 (4): 601–24.

Holman, Mirya R., and Anna Mahoney. 2018. "Stop, Collaborate, and Listen: Women's Collaboration in U.S. State Legislatures." *Legislative Studies Quarterly* 43 (2): 179–206.

Holman, M., J. L. Merolla, and E. J. Zechmeister. 2011. "Sex, Stereotypes, and Security: A Study of the Effects of Terrorist Threat on Assessments of Female Leadership." *Journal of Women in Politics* 32: 173–92.

Holman, Mirya, Jennifer L. Merolla, and Elizabeth J. Zechmeister. 2016. "Terrorist Threat, Male Stereotypes, and Candidate Evaluations." *Political Research Quarterly* 69 (1): 134–47.

Holman, Mirya R., and Monica C. Schneider. 2018. "Gender, Race, and Political Ambition: How Intersectionality and Frames Influence Interest in Political Office." *Politics, Groups, and Identities* 6 (2): 264–80.

Huddy, Lioni, and Nayda Terkildsen. 1993. "The Consequences of Gender Stereotypes for Women Candidates at Different Levels and Types of Office." *Political Research Quarterly* 46 (3): 503–25.

Hughes, Melanie. 2011. "Intersectionality, Quotas, and Minority Women's Political Representation Worldwide." *American Political Science Review* 105 (3): 604–20.

Jaffe, Alexandra. 2016. "Donald Trump Has 'Small Hands,' Marco Rubio Says." *NBCNews.com*, February 29. https://www.nbcnews.com/politics/2016-election/donald-trump-has-small-hands-marco-rubio-says-n527791

Jamieson, Kathleen H. 1995. *Beyond the Double Bind: Women and Leadership.* New York: Oxford University Press.

Jennings, M. Kent, and Richard G. Niemi. 2014. *Generations and Politics: A Panel Study of Young Adults and Their Parents.* Princeton: Princeton University Press.

Johnson, Jenna. 2016. "Donald Trump Repeats Crowd Member's Ted Cruz Insult: 'He's a Pussy.'" *Washington Post*, February 8. https://www.washingtonpost.com/news/post-politics/wp/2016/02/08/donald-trump-repeats-crowd-members-ted-cruz-insult-hes-a-pussy/

Jones, Brett D., Marie C. Paretti, Serge F. Hein, and Tamara W. Knott. 2010. "An

Analysis of Motivation Constructs with First Year Engineering Students: Relationships among Expectancies, Values, Achievement, and Career Plans." *Journal of Engineering Education* 99 (4): 319–36.

Jones-Correa, Michael. 2005. "Bringing Outsiders In." In *The Politics of Democratic Inclusion*, edited by Christina Wolbrecht and Rodney Hero. Philadelphia: Temple University Press.

Juenke, Eric Gonzalez, and Robert R. Preuhs. 2012. "Irreplaceable Legislators? Rethinking Minority Representatives in the New Century." *American Journal of Political Science* 56 (3): 705–15.

Juenke, E. G., and P. Shah. 2016. "Demand and Supply: Racial and Ethnic Minority Candidates in White Districts." *Journal of Race, Ethnicity and Politics* 1 (1): 60–90.

Kahn, Kim Fridkin. 1996. *The Political Consequences of Being a Woman*. New York: Columbia University Press.

Kanthak, Kristin, and Jonathan Woon. 2015. "Women Don't Run? Election Aversion and Candidate Entry." *American Journal of Political Science* 59 (3): 595–612.

Karpowitz, Christopher F., J. Quin Monson, and Jessica Robinson Preece. 2017. "How to Elect More Women: Gender and Candidate Success in a Field Experiment." *American Journal of Political Science* 61 (4): 927–43.

Kathlene, Lyn. 1994. "Power and Influence in State Legislatures: The Interaction of Gender and Position in Committee Hearing Debates." *American Political Science Review* 88 (3): 560–76.

Keener, Emily, JoNell Strough, and Lisa DiDonato. 2012. "Gender Differences and Similarities in Strategies for Managing Conflict with Friends and Romantic Partners." *Sex Roles* 67 (1–2): 83–97.

King, Cheryl S. 1995. "Sex-Role Identity and Decision Styles: How Gender Helps Explain the Paucity of Women at the Top." In *Gender Power, Leadership, and Governance*, edited by Georgia Duerst-Lahti and Rita Mae Kelly. Ann Arbor: University of Michigan Press.

King, Josh. 2013. "Dukakis and the Tank: The Inside Story of the Worst Campaign Photo Op Ever." *Politico.com*, November 17. https://www.politico.com/magazine/story/2013/11/dukakis-and-the-tank-099119

Kirpatrick, Jeane. 1974. *Political Woman*. New York: Basic Books.

Koenig, Alice M., Alice H. Eagly, Abigail A. Mitchell, and Tiina Ristikari. 2011. "Are Leader Stereotypes Masculine? A Meta-Analysis of Three Research Paradigms." *Psychological Bulletin* 137 (4): 616–42.

Kruse, Michael. 2018. "'A Little Errol Morris. And a Little Roger Ailes.' How a Democratic Ad Maker's Viral Videos Are Rewriting the Rules of Launching Long-Shot Candidacies." *Politico.com*, July 8. https://www.politico.com/magazine/story/2018/07/08/a-little-errol-morris-and-a-little-roger-ailes-218956

Kunovich, Sheri, and Pamela Paxton. 2005. "Pathways to Power: The Role of Political Parties in Women's National Political Representation." *American Journal of Sociology* 111 (2): 505–52.

Lane, Kristin, Jin X. Goh, and Erin Driver-Linn. 2012. "Implicit Science Stereotypes Mediate the Relationship between Gender and Academic Participation." *Sex Roles* 66 (3–4): 220–34.

Lane, Robert E. 1962. *Political Ideology: Why the American Common Man Believes What He Does*. New York: Free Press of Glencoe.

Lasswell, Howard D. 1930. *Psychopathology and Politics*. Chicago: University of Chicago Press.

Lawless, Jennifer L. 2004. "Women, War, and Winning Elections: Gender Stereotyping in the Post–September 11th Era." *Political Research Quarterly* 57 (3): 479–90.

Lawless, Jennifer L. 2012. *Becoming a Candidate: Political Ambition and the Decision to Run for Office*. New York: Cambridge University Press.

Lawless, Jennifer L., and Richard L. Fox. 2010. *It Still Takes a Candidate: Why Women Don't Run for Office*. New York: Cambridge University Press.

Lawless, Jennifer L., and Richard L. Fox. 2012. *Men Rule: The Continued Under-Representation of Women in U.S. Politics*. Washington, DC: Women and Politics Institute.

Lawless, Jennifer L., and Kathryn Pearson. 2008. "The Primary Reason for Women's Underrepresentation? Reevaluating the Conventional Wisdom." *Journal of Politics* 70 (1): 67–82.

Lawless, Jennifer L., Sean M. Theriault, and Samantha Guthrie. 2018. "Nice Girls? Sex, Collegiality, and Bipartisan Cooperation in the US Congress." *Journal of Politics* 80 (4): 1268–82.

Livingston, Robert W., Ashleigh Shelby Rosette, and Ella F. Washington. 2012. "Can an Agentic Black Woman Get Ahead? The Impact of Race and Interpersonal Dominance on Perceptions of Female Leaders." *Psychological Science* 23 (4): 354–58.

Lowande, Kenneth, Melinda Richie, and Erinn Lauterbach. 2019. "Descriptive and Substantive Representation in Congress: Evidence from 80,000 Congressional Inquiries." *American Journal of Political Science* 63 (3): 644–59.

Maestas, Cherie D., Sarah A. Fulton, Sandy L. Maisel, and Walter J. Stone. 2006. "When to Risk It? Institutions, Ambitions, and the Decision to Run for the US House." *American Political Science Review* 100 (2): 195–208.

Matsunaga, Masaki. 2010. "How to Factor-Analyze Your Data Right: Do's, Don'ts, and How-to's." *International Journal of Psychological Research* 3 (1): 97–110.

Mayer, Jeremy D., and Heather M. Schmidt. 2004. "Gendered Political Socialization in Four Contexts: Political Interest and Values among Junior High School Students in China, Japan, Mexico, and the United States." *Social Science Journal* 41 (3): 393–407.

McDermott, Monika L. 2016. *Masculinity, Femininity, and American Political Behavior*. Oxford: Oxford University Press.

Mo, Cecilia Hyunjung, Katharine M. Conn, and Georgia Anderson-Nilsson. 2019. "Youth National Service and Women's Political Ambition: The Case of Teach for America." *Politics, Groups, and Identities* 7, no. 4: 864–77. https://doi.org/10.1080/21565503.2019.1630288

Moncrief, Gary F., Peverill Squire, and Malcolm E. Jewell. 2001. *Who Runs for the Legislature?* Upper Saddle River, NJ: Prentice-Hall.

Mondak, Jeffery J. 2010. *Personality and the Foundations of Political Behavior*. Cambridge: Cambridge University Press.

Niven, David. 1998. "Party Elites and Women Candidates: The Shape of Bias." *Women and Politics* 19: 57–80.

Norris, Pippa. 1997. "Introduction: Theories of Recruitment." In *Passages to Power:*

Legislative Recruitment in Advanced Democracies, edited by Pippa Norris, 1–14. Cambridge: Cambridge University Press.

Norris, Pippa, and Joni Lovenduski. 1995. *Political Recruitment: Gender, Race and Class in the British Parliament*. New York: Cambridge University Press.

Nosek, Brian A., Mahzarin R. Banaji, and Anthony G. Greenwald. 2002. "Math = Male, Me = Female, Therefore Math Not = Me." *Journal of Personality and Social Psychology* 83: 44–59.

O'Brien, Diana Z., and Johanna Rickne. 2016. "Gender Quotas and Women's Political Leadership." *American Political Science Review* 110 (1): 112–26.

Offermann, Lynn R., and Meredith Coates. 2018. "Implicit Theories of Leadership: Stability and Change over Two Decades." *Leadership Studies* 29 (4): 513–22.

Ono, Yoshikuni, and Barry C. Burden. 2018. "The Contingent Effects of Candidate Sex on Voter Choice." *Political Behavior* 41, no. 3: 583–607. https://doi.org/10.1007/s11109-018-9464-6

Palmer, Barbara, and Dennis Simon. 2008. *Breaking the Political Glass Ceiling: Women and Congressional Elections*. New York: Routledge.

Palmieri, Jennifer. 2018. Interview with *The West Wing Weekly* Podcast. June 26. Transcripts. https://static1.squarespace.com/static/56e27eb82fe131d8eec3a4e3/t/5 bf1b65d352f533b08c91a80/1542567518531/5.05+-+Constituency+of+One. pdf

Parker, Kim, and Wendy Wang. 2013. "Modern Parenthood. Roles of Moms and Dads Converge as They Balance Work and Family." *Pew Research Social and Demographic Trends*. www.pewsocialtrends.org

Pate, Jennifer, and Richard L. Fox. 2018. "Getting Past the Gender Gap in Political Ambition." *Journal of Economic Behavior and Organization* 156: 116–83.

Paulhus, D. L., and O. P. John. 1998. "Egoistic and Moralistic Biases in Self-Perception: The Interplay of Self-Deceptive Styles with Basic Traits and Motives." *Journal of Personality* 66: 1025–60.

Pearson, Kathryn, and Eric McGhee. 2013. "What It Takes to Win: Questioning 'Gender Neutral' Outcomes in US House Elections." *Politics and Gender* 9 (4): 439–62.

Petrocik, John, R. 1996. "Issue Ownership in Presidential Elections, with a 1980 Case Study." *American Journal of Political Science* 40 (3): 825–59.

Preece, Jessica, and Olga Bogach Stoddard. 2015. "Does the Message Matter? A Field Experiment on Political Party Recruitment." *Journal of Experimental Political Science* 2 (1): 26–35.

Preece, Jessica Robinson, Olga Bogach Stoddard, and Rachel Fisher. 2016. "Run, Jane, Run! Gendered Responses to Political Party Recruitment." *Political Behavior* 38: 561–77.

Prinz, Timothy S. 1993. "The Career Paths of Elected Politicians: A Review and Prospectus." In *Ambition and Beyond: Career Paths of American Politicians*, edited by Shirley Williams and E. L. Lasher, 11–63. Berkeley: Institute of Governmental Studies, UC Berkeley.

Pruysers, Scott, and Julie Blais. 2019. "Narcissistic Women and Cash-Strapped Men: Who Can Be Encouraged to Consider Running for Political Office and Who Should Do the Encouraging?" *Political Research Quarterly* 72 (1): 229–42.

Ratcliffe, R. G. 2018. "Viral Video Gives Democrat MJ Hegar a Big Financial Boost

Against Republican Congressman John Carter." *Texas Monthly*, July 10. https://www.texasmonthly.com/politics/viral-video-gives-democrat-mj-hegar-big-financial-boost-republican-congressman-john-carter/

Roberts, Damon C., and Stephen M. Utych. 2020. "Linking Gender, Language, and Partisanship: Developing a Database of Masculine and Feminine Words." *Political Research Quarterly* 73 (1): 40–50.

Rohde, David W. 1979. "Risk-Bearing and Progressive Ambition: The Case of Members of the United States House of Representatives." *American Journal of Political Science* 23 (1): 1–26.

Rosenthal, Cindy Simon. 2000. "Gender Styles in State Legislatures." *Women & Politics* 21 (2): 21–45.

Rosenwasser, Shirley M., and Norma G. Dean. 1989. "Gender Role and Political Office: Effects of Perceived Masculinity/Femininity of Candidate and Political Office." *Psychology of Women Quarterly* 13 (1): 77–85.

Rudman, L. A., C. A. Moss-Racusin, J. E. Phelan, and S. Nauts. 2012. "Status Incongruity and Backlash Effects: Defending the Gender Hierarchy Motivates Prejudice against Female Leaders." *Journal of Experimental Social Psychology* 48 (1): 165–79.

Sanbonmatsu, Kira. 2002. "Political Parties and the Recruitment of Women to State Legislatures." *Journal of Politics* 64 (3): 791–809.

Sanbonmatsu, Kira. 2006. *Where Women Run: Gender and Party in the American States.* Ann Arbor: University of Michigan Press.

Sanbonmatsu, Kira. 2015. "Electing Women of Color: The Role of Campaign Trainings." *Journal of Women, Politics and Policy* 36 (2): 137–60.

Sanbonmatsu, Kira, and Susan J. Carroll. 2017. "Women's Decisions to Run for Office: A Relationally Embedded Model." In *The Political Psychology of Women in U.S. Politics*, edited by A. L. Bos and M. C. Schneider, 148–64. New York: Routledge.

Sanbonmatsu, Kira, Susan J. Carroll, and Debbie Walsh. 2009. *Poised to Run: Women's Pathways to the State Legislatures.* New Brunswick, NJ: Center for American Women and Politics, Rutgers University.

Sanbonmatsu, Kira, and Kathleen A. Dolan. 2009. "Do Gender Stereotypes Transcend Party?" *Political Research Quarterly* 62 (3): 485–94.

Sapiro, Virginia. 1981. "If U.S. Senator Baker Were a Woman: An Experimental Study of Candidate Images." *Political Psychology* 3 (1–2): 61–83.

Schleifer, Theodore. 2015. "Rick Perry's Tough Guy Challenge for Donald Trump." *CNN.com*, July 30. https://www.cnn.com/2015/07/29/politics/rick-perry-donald-trump-pull-up-contest/

Schlesinger, Joseph A. 1966. *Ambition and Politics.* Chicago: Rand McNally.

Schneider, Monica C. 2014. "The Effects of Gender-Bending on Candidate Evaluations." *Journal of Women, Politics and Policy* 35 (1): 55–77.

Schneider, Monica C., and Angela L. Bos. 2014. "Measuring Stereotypes of Female Politicians." *Political Psychology* 35 (2): 245–66.

Schneider, Monica C., and Angela Bos. 2019. "The Application of Social Role Theory to the Study of Gender in Politics." *Political Psychology*, March 20. https://doi.org/10.1111/pops.12573

Schneider, Monica C., Mirya R. Holman, Amanda B. Diekman, and Thomas

McAndrew. 2016. "Power, Conflict, and Community: How Gendered Views of Political Power Influence Women's Political Ambition." *Political Psychology* 37 (4): 515–31.

Scott, Jamil S. 2018. "Ambition Is Not Enough: Explaining Candidate Emergence in State Level Politics." PhD diss., Michigan State University. https://search. proquest.com/openview/c36ebaf6d9c05c41345def000ae03504/1?pq-origsite= gscholar&cbl=18750&diss=y

Seltzer, Richard A., Jody Newman, and Melissa Vorhees Leighton. 1997. *Sex as a Political Variable: Women as Candidates and Voters in US Elections*. Boulder, CO: Lynne Rienner.

Shah, Paru. 2014. "It Takes a Black Candidate: A Supply-Side Theory of Minority Representation." *Political Research Quarterly* 67 (2): 266–79.

Shah, Paru. 2015. "Stepping Up: Black Political Ambition and Success." *Politics, Groups, and Identities* 3 (2): 278–94.

Shah, Paru, Jamil Scott, and Eric Gonzalez Juenke. 2019. "Women of Color Candidates: Examining Emergence and Success in State Legislative Elections." *Politics Groups and Identities* 7 (2): 429–43.

Shames, Shauna L. 2014. "The Rational Non-Candidate: A Theory of (Uneven) Candidate Deterrence." PhD diss, Harvard University.

Shames, Shauna L. 2017. *Out of the Running: Why Millennials Reject Political Careers and Why It Matters*. New York: New York University Press.

Silberman, Rachel. 2015. "Gender Roles, Work-Life Balance, and Running for Office." *Quarterly Journal of Political Science* 10 (2): 123–53.

Silva, Andrea, and Carrie Skulley. 2018. "Always Running: Candidate Emergence among Women of Color over Time." *Political Research Quarterly* 72 (2): 342–59.

Snowe, Olympia. 2012. "Olympia Snowe: Why I'm Leaving the Senate." *Washington Post*, March 1. https://www.washingtonpost.com/opinions/olym pia-snowe-why-im-leaving-the-senate/2012/03/01/gIQApGYZlR_story. html?noredirect=onandutm_term=.7c88abfab19c

Spence, Janet T. 1993. "Gender-Related Traits and Gender Ideology: Evidence for a Multifactorial Theory." *Journal of Personality and Social Psychology* 64 (4): 624–35.

Spence, Janet T. 2011. "Off with the Old, on with the New." *Psychology of Women Quarterly* 35: 504–9.

Spence, Janet T., and Camille E. Buckner. 2000. "Instrumental and Expressive Traits, Trait Stereotypes, and Sexist Attitudes: What Do They Signify?" *Psychology of Women Quarterly* 24: 44–62.

Spence, Janet T., and Robert L. Helmreich. 1978. *Masculinity and Femininity: Their Psychological Dimensions, Correlates, and Antecedents*. Austin: University of Texas Press.

Spence, Janet T., Robert L. Helmreich, and Joy Stapp. 1975. "Ratings of Self and Peers on Sex Role Attributes and Their Relation to Self-Esteem and Conceptions of Masculinity and Femininity." *Journal of Personality and Social Psychology* 32 (1): 29–39.

Stalsburg, Brittany L. 2010. "Voting for Mom: The Political Consequences of Being a Parent for Male and Female Candidates." *Politics and Gender* 6: 373–404.

Stalsburg, Brittany L., and Mona S. Kleinberg. 2015. "'A Mom First and a Candidate Second': Gender Differences in Candidates' Self-Presentation of Family." *Journal of Political Marketing* 15 (4): 285–310.

Streb, Matthew J., Barbara Burrell, Brian Frederick, and Michael A. Genovese. 2008. "Social Desirability Effects and Support for a Female American President." *Public Opinion Quarterly* 72 (1): 76–89.

Strolovitch, Dara Z. 2007. *Affirmative Advocacy: Race, Class, and Gender in Interest Group Politics*. Chicago: University of Chicago Press.

Svara, James H. 2003. *Two Decades of Continuity and Change in American City Councils*. www.nlc.org/resources_for_cities/publications/1637.aspx

Sweet-Cushman, Jennie. 2018. "Where Does the Pipeline Get Leaky? The Progressive Ambition of School Board Members and Personal and Political Network Recruitment." *Politics, Groups, and Identities*, November 8. https://doi.org/10.1080/21565503.2018.1541417

Swers, Michele L. 2002. *The Difference Women Make*. Chicago: University of Chicago.

Swers, Michele L. 2005. "Connecting Descriptive and Substantive Representation: An Analysis of Sex Differences in Cosponsorship Activity." *Legislative Studies Quarterly* 30 (3): 407–33.

Swers, Michele L. 2013. *Women in the Club: Gender and Policy Making in the Senate*. Chicago: University of Chicago Press.

Swers, Michele L. 2016. "Pursuing Women's Interests in Partisan Times: Explaining Gender Differences in Legislative Activity on Health, Education, and Women's Health Issues." *Journal of Women, Politics and Policy* 37 (3): 249–73.

Swigger, Nathaniel, and Meredith Meyer. 2018. "Gender Essentialism and Responses to Candidates' Messages." *Political Psychology*, November 25. https://doi.org/10.1111/pops.12556

Teele, Dawn Langan, Joshua Kalla, and Frances Rosenbluth. 2018. "The Ties That Double Bind: Social Roles and Women's Underrepresentation in Politics." *American Political Science Review* 112 (3): 525–41.

Thomas, Melanee, and Amanda Bittner. 2017. "The 'Mommy Problem'? Gender, Parental Status, and Politics." In *Mothers and Others: The Role of Parenthood in Politics*, edited by Melanee Thomas and Amanda Bittner. Vancouver, BC, Canada: UBC Press.

Thomas, Sue. 1992. "The Effects of Race and Gender on Constituency Service." *Western Political Quarterly* 45 (1): 169–80.

Thomas, Sue. 1994. *How Women Legislate*. New York: Oxford University Press.

Thomas, Sue. 2002. "The Personal Is the Political: Antecedents of Gendered Choices of Elected Representatives." *Sex Roles* 47 (7–8): 343–53.

Thomas, Sue. 2005. "Introduction: Women and Elective Office: Past, Present, and Future." In *Women and Elective Office*, 2nd ed., edited by Sue Thomas and Clyde Wilcox, 3–25. New York: Oxford University Press.

Thomsen, Danielle M. 2017. *Opting Out of Congress: Partisan Polarization and the Decline of Moderate Candidates*. Cambridge: Cambridge University Press.

Thomsen, Danielle M., and Michele L. Swers. 2017. "Which Women Can Run?

Gender, Partisanship and Candidate Donor Networks." *Political Research Quarterly* 70 (2): 449–63.

Tolleson-Rinehart, Sue. 1991. "Do Women Leaders Make a Difference? Substance, Style, and Perceptions." In *Gender and Policymaking: Studies of Women in Office*, edited by Debra Dodson. New Brunswick, NJ: Rutgers University.

Tomasky, Michael. 2012. "Mitt Romney: A Candidate with a Serious Wimp Problem." *Newsweek*, July 29.

Trapnell, Paul D., and Delroy L. Paulhus. 2012. "Agentic and Communal Values: Their Scope and Measurement." *Journal of Personality Assessment* 94 (1): 39–52.

Twenge, Jean M. 1997. "Changes in Masculine and Feminine Traits over Time: A Meta-Analysis." *Sex Roles* 36 (5–6): 305–25.

Twenge, Jean M. 2001. "Changes in Women's Assertiveness in Response to Status and Roles: A Cross-Temporal Meta-Analysis." *Journal of Personality and Social Psychology* 81: 133–45.

Vecchio, Robert P. 2002. "Leadership and Gender Advantage." *Leadership Quarterly* 13 (6): 643–71.

Verba, Sidney, Kay Lehman Schlozman, and Henry E. Brady. 1995. *Voice and Equality: Civic Voluntarism in American Politics*. Cambridge: Harvard University Press.

Vinnicombe, Susan, and Val Singh. 2002. "Women-Only Management Training: An Essential Part of Women's Leadership Development." *Journal of Change Management* 3 (4): 294–306.

Ward, Charles L., Beverly E. Thorn, Kristi L. Clements, Kim E. Dixon, and Stacy D. Sanford. 2006. "Measurement of Agency, Communion, and Emotional Vulnerability with the Personal Attributes Questionnaire." *Journal of Personality Assessment* 86 (2): 206–16.

Warner, Margaret G. 1987. "Bush Battles the 'Wimp Factor.'" *Newsweek*, October 19.

Warren, Howard C., and Leonard Carmichael. 1930. *Elements of Human Psychology*. New York: Houghton Mifflin.

Welch, Susan. 1978. "Recruitment of Women to Public Office: A Discriminant Analysis." *Western Political Quarterly* 31 (3): 372–80.

Windett, Jason. 2014. "Differing Paths to the Top: Gender, Ambition, and Running for Governor." *Journal of Women, Politics and Policy* 35 (4): 287–314.

Winter, Nicholas J. G. 2010. "Masculine Republicans and Feminine Democrats: Gender and Americans' Explicit and Implicit Images of the Political Parties." *Political Behavior* 32 (4): 587–618.

Wolbrecht, Christina, and Rodney Hero. 2005. *The Politics of Democratic Inclusion*. Philadelphia: Temple University Press.

Women's Media Center. 2017. "The Status of Women in U.S Media 2017." http://www.womensmediacenter.com/assets/site/reports/10c550d19ef9f3688f_mlbres2jd.pdf

Wood, J. Luke, Frank Harris III, and Christopher B. Newman. 2015. "An Exploratory Investigation of the Effect of Racial and Masculine Identity on Focus: An Examination of White, Black, Mexicano, Latino, and Asian Men in Community Colleges." *Culture, Society, and Masculinities* 7 (1): 61–72.

Wood, Wendy, and Alice Eagly. 2002. A Cross-Cultural Analysis of the Behavior of Women and Men: Implications for the origins of Sex Differences." *Psychological Bulletin* 128: 699–727.

Yoder, Jan D., Robert W. Rice, Jerome Adams, Robert F. Priest, and Howard T. Prince II. 1982. "Reliability of the Attitudes toward Women Scale and the Personal Attributes Questionnaire (PAQ)." *Sex Roles* 8 (6): 651–57.

Index

153